Revelation

Inspiration

Memories

Latena Willis

Order this book online at www.trafford.com
or email orders@trafford.com

Most Trafford titles are also available at major online book retailers.

Printed in the United States of America.

ISBN: 978-1-4269-5484-9 (sc)
ISBN: 978-1-4269-5485-6 (e)

Trafford rev. 11/13/2013

 www.trafford.com

North America & international
toll-free: 1 888 232 4444 (USA & Canada)
fax: 812 355 4082

Contents

Foreword

It was in the month of June just before my fourteenth birthday, when my mother took us boys to a new church in our small town of Harrisburg, Oregon. On that Sunday is when I first saw Latena Anglin, who had just come from Oklahoma and was attending this church for the first time.

We both graduated from Harrisburg High School in 1952 and were married on January 10, 1954. We have known one another since age thirteen and I continually thank God for allowing us to live our lives together, and serve him together all these years.

Latena has always been a gifted person in wisdom, intelligence and in spiritual things. She has manifested exceptional commitment to the Lord and His service. Over the years she has proven herself to be trustworthy and filled with compassion for others.

As a Pastor's wife she has represented me with honor in whatever she has done and wherever she has gone. She has handled the difficulties of life with perseverance and patience. The duties of a Pastor's wife are very demanding both in public and private. There have been frequent times when visitors have shown up without warning and she has graciously entertained them, fed them and arranged sleeping quarters for them at the expense of our two children. Besides being a full time Pastor's wife and mother, she has worked outside the home continually, supplementing our income.

Even while pastoring the Valley Christian Center in Harrisburg, Oregon, we began traveling with our church teenagers in outreach missions throughout the Northwest. Somewhere in the mid-seventies we began ministering in Indian villages in Northern British Colombia of Canada. The trips were mostly in the winter season so we had to endure the snow and ice. Latena never faltered, endured the hardships, and became a positive influence in the lives of others. Later in 1983 we began traveling to the Philippines to minister. This has continued over the last 26 years. She met every challenge with grace, went through the hardships and the dangers with a praise on her lips and determination in her heart. Words fail me in trying to explain my appreciation for her unquestioned loyalty to the ministry. She has faithfully supported me, taught her personal revelations and expounded the word to thousands of hungry people. In 1997 we traveled together to Ghana and Togo, West Africa. Together we blazed a trail for others to follow.

Through the years God has given to her special revelations, also she has written articles of wisdom that are so helpful to others. I felt it was important to organize her writings into a book so others could more fully appreciate her life-time contribution to the work of the kingdom of God.

Latena is an example of the grace of God in action, and she is appreciated by me and the family so much. As you read this book, I am confident you will meet the heart of a servant of the Lord, and your life will be changed.

Husband and Preacher
Leon C Willis

Discerning the Body
of Christ

The Lord gave me a dream. Our church was having many problems. Several had left for various reasons. I dreamed that a few of us agreed that we would begin to praise the Lord daily in whatever we would be doing. Not asking Him for anything - only giving Him blessing and praise for all He has already done...voicing our appreciation to Him. As we began to do this, we found not only were we giving our praise upward toward God, but outward to each other. Our praise and appreciation not only for the Lord, but for each other began to grow as we learned to "discern" the body of Christ. We recognized Jesus in each life as we started to bless and praise (say good things about) each other. It is okay to praise each other because as I stated, we see Jesus and His works in each person. We **worship** only the Lord. It does not work for us to bless and praise the Lord and criticize each other. We cannot expect to have God's approval. We cannot be faithful to the Lord and not be faithful to the body that He has placed us in. If we take our sacrifice (of praise) to the altar and remember that we are not in fellowship with another, we must leave our sacrifice and go to our brother or sister and then return to offer our praise to the Lord.

The church is characterized in several different ways in the Bible... when we are speaking of warfare, the Church is an army; in intimacy

- the Bride; in structure - the Temple; functioning - the Body and it is this, the Body, that I want to address today.

"...that there should be no division in the body, but that the member should have the same care for one another. Now you are Christ's body and individually members of it" (1 Cor.12:25-27).

Relationships within the body of Christ are so important! Too often, people leave our churches because of hurts inside by other Christians. WE NEED TO MAKE *"STAYING IN THE BODY"* A SAFE PLACE TO BE. The Church is referred to as the spiritual body of Christ. When Paul was writing to the church at Corinth, he was addressing "problems in the body".

Paul was writing to Christians!

"I do not praise you because you come together not for the better but for the worse....when you come together as a church, I hear that divisions exist among you..." (1 Cor.11:17).

"I am afraid that when I come to you, I will find strife, jealousy, angry tempers, disputes, slanders, gossip, arrogance, disturbances" (2 Cor.12:20).

EVEN IN THE GALATIAN CHURCH:

"...if you bite and devour one another, you will be consumed by one another." (Gal.5:15).

AND THE EPHESIAN CHURCH

"Let no unwholesome word proceed from your mouth...do not grieve the Holy Spirit of God...let all bitterness (sharp, harsh, long term disagreements, resentful, cynical) and wrath (reaction to bitterness) and anger (sudden anger - temper) and clamor (demand or complaint) and slander (an utterance that damages another's reputation) be put away from you with all malice (active ill-will). Be kind to one another, tender-hearted, forgiving each other, just as God in Christ also has forgiven you" (Eph.4:29-32).

JAMES ADDRESSED THE PROBLEM:

"...where jealousy and selfish ambition exist, there is disorder and every evil thing." (James 3:16).

"Jesus took the bread and broke it and said, "This is my body, which is for you; do this in remembrance of Me. He took the cup also, saying, this is the cup of the new covenant in My blood, do this as often as you drink it in remembrance of Me" (1Cor.11:24). (verses 28,29) *"For he who eats and drinks, eats and drinks judgment to himself if he does not (discern) judge the body rightly." (verse 30)"For this reason many among you are weak and sick and a number* sleep."

Something was lacking in the Corinthian, Galatian, and Ephesian Churches and something is still lacking in our churches today!! Do you suppose it just might be a discernment problem?

In contrast to the New Testament churches, in which there were many weak and sick (and their number was small in comparison) there was a much larger church, about 3 million, yet there was not a feeble one among them! It was the children of Israel when they were leaving Egypt. Their covenant was established by the blood of a lamb. The New Testament covenant was established by the Blood of the Son of God. Why were they all healed, and the New Testament Churches then as well as today still have people sick and dying in them as well as personality conflicts.

The children of Israel were 400 years in Egypt and spent years crying out to God for deliverance and one day God heard them and He remembered His covenant with Abraham and Isaac and Jacob.... and He had respect toward them and He sent Moses. After some very eventful times in Egypt, God spoke to Moses, *"Speak to all the congregation of Israel saying, take to them every man a lamb and kill it, and take the blood, and strike it on the two side posts and on the upper door post of the houses, and eat the flesh of the lamb, it is the Lord's Passover"* (Ex 12:3).

Two things to do: apply the blood and eat the flesh.

First: A lamb was to be slain and its blood was to be applied to the door posts of each house (God's covenant of protection). The blood shall be for you a token upon the houses where you are and when I see the blood, I will pass over you and the plague will not come upon you to destroy you. This represented, in type, our identification by faith with the blood of Jesus, our Lamb. *"Being now justified by His blood, we shall be saved from the wrath to come"* (Rom 5:9).

Second: Each Israelite was to eat the lamb's flesh, appropriating physical strength for the journey. Eating the lamb had nothing to do with the passing of the destroyer. The blood was a signal or sign that the destroyer had no authority to touch that house.

Israel was beginning a journey, which was a type of our Christian journey through life. God planned that His children be well and strong for this journey and that is still His plan! <u>What happened when the Israelites ate the flesh of the lamb? God has installed in the human body a processing plant which we call a stomach. The food we eat is digested there and sent out into our bloodstream. Its chemical essence becomes flesh of our flesh, bone of our bone, skin of our skin, body of our body. It becomes a part of us.</u> As we partake of the Body of Christ in a spiritual sense, by faith we receive Him and it is His blood that flows through our veins. We become flesh of His flesh, bone of His bone, skin of His skin and in Him there is total health....BODY, SOUL, AND SPIRIT.

THE FLESH OF THE LAMB SLAIN IN EGYPT WHEN EATEN, became a part of each Israelite. It was a type of the body of Jesus Christ, God's Son who was to be slain for the whole world. *"I am the bread of life"* (St John 6:48).*(* verse 54)**...** *whoever eats my flesh and drinks my blood has eternal life.....(*verse 56)**...** *"he who eats my flesh and drinks my blood abides in Me"*. Paul said that we, by faith, have become members of His body, His flesh and His bones. Eph 5:30 The Israelites ate the lamb's body and began their journey the next day. As they journeyed, their sicknesses banished and their infirmities disappeared. They were physically strong and whole. There was not one feeble person among them!

How do we eat and drink of the Lord's body today? All of us have participated in the ceremony of "The Lord's Table" and been told to "search our hearts". I have asked the Lord to help me and I believe He has given me a revelation concerning partaking of the Lord's body in a spiritual sense.

SPIRITUAL NUTRITION FOR THE SPIRIT MAN

Comparing the natural nutrition with the believer's spiritual nutrition

I believe when our spiritual appetite is awakened to the word of God and we begin to search the scriptures for the will of God , we are eating of His body. This is our **SPIRITUAL PROTEIN** to make us strong, to help us grow, give us energy and help us fight fleshly attacks or sinful infections. Diet is what we eat, nutrition is that which our cells actually receive and our cells cannot receive nourishment without enzymes (small protein molecules which carry nutrition to the cells of our bodies). Enzymes must be present for digestion. Our **SPIRITUAL ENZYMES** are our prayer and meditation. After eating the word of God, we need to allow time for it to "roll around " on the inside of us so it can be digested, assimilated as it is circulated by our blood stream to nourish our cells and to produce in us a changed nature.

Our **SPIRITUAL VITAMINS AND MINERALS** are received from our times of praise and worship and fellowship. Just as natural vitamins and minerals speed healing, help to build and repair tissue, help nerves and other functions to perform, we must have times of praise, worship and fellowship with the rest of the body in order to be spiritually healthy. Especially when we have received an injury, we need to allow the rest of the body to minister healing. Body ministry is so important. Too much of the time during discouragement, or being overtaken in a fault, the first thing we want to do is to leave the church body. That is not the time to leave, but to stay and allow healing to take place. You will be strengthened by the body ministry.

LIPID (oil) is necessary in the body to keep our cells soft and pliable in order to take in nutrition and to eliminate waste. The Holy Spirit is our oil. With the Holy Spirit controlling our lives and censoring our thought-life, we are able to pass many things on by as waste and not allow it to indwell us or to become a part of our nature. Just as disease in our natural body begins with a single cell, sin begins with a single thought. We need the Holy Spirit active in our lives. Without the Holy Spirit control, we will become hardened and given to our own pleasures and desires. With the Holy Spirit censoring our thought life, we are also able to pass many things on by as waste and not allow it to indwell us or become a part of our natures. The Holy Spirit is not an option for a Christian it is a must!

CARBOHYDRATES supply energy and helps the body use other nutrients. Our SPIRITUAL CARBOHYDRATES are our 5 senses, our soul, that which contains our thoughts, feelings and emotions. Natural quality carbohydrates are grains, fruits, vegetables. This will cause a steady flow of energy that is healthy. Many carbohydrates are "empty calories" filled with fat and refined sugar. This gives a feeling of fullness but has no long lasting results, gives a quick energy with a "high" then a "low". When our feelings, mind, emotions are in line with the word of God and we are controlled by His will, we are taking in our spiritual quality nutrients. If we live on soulish experiences and continually look for ways to satisfy our "sweet tooth", our spiritual nature will be moody and changeable and will not have long lasting results. We will not experience a changed nature. This person will have a "roller coaster" Christianity, sometimes going from place to place, looking for sugar coated ministries, never being satisfied and never reaching spiritual maturity.

WATER - Water is not only the most abundant nutrient found in the body, it also is by far the most important nutrient. It is responsible for and involved in nearly every body process, including digestion, absorption, circulation and excretion. Water is the primary transporter of nutrients throughout the body and is necessary for all building functions in the body. Water helps maintain a normal body temperature and is essential for carrying waste material out of the body. Water helps to maintain proper muscle tone and prevents dehydration. When our body gets the water it needs to function, its fluids are perfectly balanced and natural thirst returns. The less water you drink, the less you want to drink! We need to develop a desire for water.

I COMPARE WATER FOR THE SPIRIT MAN WITH THE ANOINTING. The word "Christ" means "the anointed one". The anointing is the element that enables us to partake of the realm of the Spiritual. When we are anointed, or in the atmosphere of the anointing, we hear with His understanding (because we have the mind of Christ). The quality of our physical life is directly related to the care and food that it has received. So also, that which we are in our spirit man must be nourished and build up. If we receive the word of God only with our minds, our spirit man is not being fed. For the ministry of the Word to become spiritual food, it must be anointed. It must come from the presence of the Lord through an anointed ministry in an atmosphere of the anointing. There must be an openness of heart and receptivity of spirit in order to receive. John 3:6 "that which is born of flesh is flesh and that which is born of Spirit is Spirit". The Lord patiently waits for His Body to grow and mature. Let us eat of the food that enables us to grow and drink plenty of His anointing water. If you do not have a spiritual desire for the things of the spirit, just begin to drink....the more you drink and eat of the Spirit, the more you will hunger and thirst for His righteousness.

Jesus said,"*My food is to do the will of the one who sent me and to accomplish His work*" (Luke 4:32-34). There is nothing that satisfies the spiritual man so totally as doing the will of God and once your taste buds have been awakened to this taste, you will long for and crave another time at the table of the Lord.

There are only two ways that we can expect to receive anything from God. That is through FAITH AND OBEDIENCE. We must be willing to adjust our wills to His will in obedience....and receive His benefits for us by faith. The Israelites believed in His power and accepted His benefits BUT they never accepted His will for them. They lived in disobedience.

I believe that partaking of the Lord's table is more than taking of the bread and wine (grape juice) in a ceremony on Sunday Morning. This is good, because we remember His provision on the cross when He paid for our salvation and our healing with His own body, but, I believe we eat/partake of the body of Christ each time we meet together with our church body and participate in praise and worship. I believe as we obey His word and practice His will in our lives, we are eating of the body of Christ. Each time we meet with Him in our closets of prayer and spend time with Him we are partaking of Him.

It is more *than* a ceremony. It is a daily communion with Him that gives us strength and causes us to be changed and takes us into a spiritual maturity.

I believe that as we discern each other as a part of that body and begin to really love each other as we love Christ, we will become that glorious Church that will show the world JESUS, the anointed one.

I believe our spiritual natures are being changed now as we practice the Word of God, and not necessarily when we "are caught up to meet Him in the air." As we are changed into His nature then we will become that glorious Church marching across the land in total health; a healed body, a restored mind and a united spirit performing the works of God.

Just as Jesus came into the world to show us the Father, Jesus sent the Holy Spirit into believers to show our world HIMSELF. "By this shall all men know that you are my disciples, because you have love one for another" (St John 13:35). The world cannot see our love for Jesus, but they can see our love for each other. *"This is my commandment that you love one another.."* (St. John 15:22). *L*ove is not a choice, but a commandment! His commandments were not given to appease our five senses but to change us as we practice His commandments. If we do not have love, then we do not have God. God's love is not based on feelings for each other but on our commitment to one another and our commitment to do the will of God. We are loving one another when we show respect, kindness and value to one another as being a part of the body of Christ, even if there may be personality problems. We can take control of our own behavior.

When Jesus was in the garden, He prayed, *"Father, if it could be your will, take this cup from me."* His feelings did not want to go to the cross! Then He said, *"Never-the-less not my will but thy will be done"*. He bypassed His feelings and as an act of obedience to the will of the Father, He went to the cross for you and me.

I believe there is healing in discerning the body of Christ! God declared that He would allow no disease to come upon the Israelites as long as they were obedient to Him. That is all he ever asked of them and that is what he is wanting from us now....OBEDIENCE.... Ex. 15:26

ALL OF GOD'S PROMISES ARE STILL OURS AND ARE READY FOR US TO CLAIM BY FAITH! Remember! Israel applied the lamb's blood to their door post - for protection (salvation) and they also ate the lamb's body - for strength (healing). Brother Osborne has made the statement that sin and sickness are Satan's twin evils, designed to tear down, to kill and to destroy the human race - God's creation. Salvation from sin and healing from sickness are God's twin mercies provided to replace these spiritual and physical evils with the abundant and miracle life of Jesus Christ in the believer's spirit and body. When Jesus became our substitute, bearing our sins and our sicknesses, He did it in order that we might be delivered from them and their power.

Deliverance from sin and sickness - a packaged deal

God places no premium on sickness and He does not want you to suffer sickness for His glory! Sickness does not glorify the Father any more than sin does. God is not purifying or glorifying His church through affliction. It is not that God is testing our faith. Sickness is due to the failure of being taught about the BODY of Christ as we have been taught about the BLOOD of Christ. In churches throughout the world Christians are suffering from diseases and sickness that Jesus Christ, our substitute, has already borne.

God was not only the deliverer from the destroyer for the Israelites, but also the healer of their diseases! Every Israelite who put the lamb's blood on the door posts was protected from the death angel....likewise....everyone who ate of the lamb's body was freed, healed, and delivered from bondage. Ps. 103 *"Bless the Lord O my soul, and forget not all His benefits. Who forgives all of my iniquities (sin question) and who heals all of my diseases (sickness question)".* Provision has been made for deliverance from both sin and sickness. *He was wounded for our transgressions, He was bruised for our iniquities (sin question) and with His stripes we are healed (sickness).*

Jesus is our Healer and our Savior

Three years of Jesus' life were occupied in healing the sick and forgiving the sinful. Then came the time he became our substitute. He became sinful with our sins and sick with our sicknesses. Both sin and sickness had to be put away ,but, first the penalty for both had to be paid! Jesus, sinless and sick-less was the only one who could do this and He did this because of His great love for you and me!

Before He went to the cross....Jesus, our lamb, was beaten, spit on, bruised, tortured. Deep furrows were plowed by the Roman lash as it tore pieces of flesh from His back. These were the stripes by which Isaiah and Peter said "we were healed". His body was brutally beaten for us. This was not the sacrifice made for our sins but the bearing of our sicknesses, so that provision could be made for the healing of our bodies. *"He himself took our infirmities and carried away our diseases"* (Matt 8:17).

Jesus, suffered intense spiritual agony at Calvary, for during that time even His Father turned away from Him. A crown of thorns was placed on His head. This was provision for the healing of our soul... our mind, will and emotions!

After they had stripped and bruised His body, then they nailed Him to the cross and pierced His side. His blood ran down on the ground - blood that was shed for many - the remission of sins. This blood was not for the healing of sickness. Matt 26:28 For this is my blood of the covenant which is poured out for many for forgiveness of sins. Jesus, our lamb suffered in three ways: He shed His blood on the cross for our salvation from sin and He bore the stripes on His body for our healing from sickness. A crown of thorns was placed on his head. This was provision for the healing of our soul...our mind, will and emotions! Let us look at some scriptures :

Isaiah 53:5 He was pierced through for our transgressions. He was crushed for our iniquities, The chastening for our well being fell upon Him, and by His scourging we are healed.

Mathew 11:28-30, Come to Me, all who are weary and heavy-laden, and I will give you rest. Take my yoke upon you and learn from Me for I am gentle and humble in heart and you shall find rest for your souls.. For My yoke is easy and my burden is light.

Philippians 4:4-9 Rejoice in the Lord always, and again I say rejoice! Let your forbearing (gentle) spirit be known to all men. The Lord is near. Be anxious for nothing, but in everything by prayer and supplication (request for spiritual benefits) with thanksgiving, let your request be made known to God. And the peace of God which surpasses all comprehension (low level thinking) shall guard (garrison, patrol, protection) your hearts and minds in Christ Jesus.

Finally, brethren, whatever is true, whatever is honorable, whatever is right, whatever is of good repute, if there is any excellence and if anything worthy of praise, let your mind dwell on these things. The things you have learned and received and heard and seen in Me, **practice** these things; and the God of peace shall be with you.

Our parts: verse 4....rejoice, verse 6...don't worry, pray verse 8... think about good things and the result is God's peace!

Jesus has completely delivered Humankind spiritually and physically and mentally from all satanic bondage. By knowing God's word we discover our deliverance from the power of sickness in our lives because of the striped (wounded) body of Christ. In the same way we learn to discern our deliverance from the power of sin in our lives because of the shed blood of Christ. Our minds are free because of the crown of thorns that He endured for us. He paid for the renewing of our minds. He has paid for the renewing of our thought patterns. We are healed, body, soul, and spirit. We are as free from sickness as we are from sin! Sickness has no more power over us than sin does. Sickness is no more for God's glory than sin is. We no more accept sickness in our lives than we accept sin. We can have the "mind of Christ". 1 Corinthians 2:16

Here are some more scriptures to encourage us:

Romans 12:2 We can be transformed by the renewing of our minds.

2 Timothy 1:7, God has not given us a spirit of timidity, but of power and love and discipline (sound judgment).

When we "miss the mark" or we are "overtaken in a fault", even though we are born again and know that we stand righteous before

13

God because of the redemptive act of Jesus, we come to Jesus, search our hearts and repent again and continue our Christian journey. We seem to always be falling short of the glory (nature and character) of God. (Rom. 3:23) We grow and learn from our mistakes. We correct the problems. Our weaknesses become our strengths as we grow into spiritual maturity. Maybe it is our thought life that needs to be disciplined. Perhaps we are walking according to the "flesh" (Galatians 5:19) It may be lack of self control. We do not give up but we make corrections and overcome the sin that would destroy us. We have the Holy Spirit in our lives and with this the power to overcome our old nature and to make right choices. There are things that are required of us to do. Eph 4:22-32 Paul said "YOU lay aside the old self ." YOU lay aside lying, lusting, temper tantrums, bitterness...... God helps us make the choices but he does not take it away. It is our job to "lay aside the old nature".

In the same way concerning sickness, first, consider this illness the enemy! Learn everything you can about it. Read! See how it works and what you have done to allow this invasion in your body! If you have been sabotaging your own body by your life style , change! If you have been withholding proper nutrition, learn what your body needs to be healthy. Educate yourself concerning nutrition, learn about "fast foods" and preservatives used in our foods today. Begin making quality choices concerning your health and your family's health. Just as we as Christians cannot live like the world lives and grow into a mature Christian, perhaps we should consider that we also cannot eat in the world's fast lane and remain healthy. Be willing to eat those foods you find less desirable because it is better for you! (Just as you keep His commandments even when you don't feel like it.) You have the power of the Holy Spirit to give you wisdom and knowledge. He will work with you as you learn about your enemy, sickness! The Lord will meet you and help you as you trust in His word. Sometimes we treat our bodies in manners that would destroy it and expect God to just keep us healthy while God has given us the intelligence to help ourselves. Many times, God has given us a miracle and healed us from a degenerative disease. We continue our life style of eating and soon we are in the same shape again and wonder where our healing went! **GOD HELP US TO USE WISDOM AND KNOWLEDGE to overcome sickness in the same way that we use God's help in overcoming sin!** God will meet us and add to us whatever we need. We must work with the Holy Spirit to reach our health potential. Wouldn't it be great, if each member of the body of Christ was the healthiest person in the world? We can be! We must assume our part of the responsibility for our health, just as we do our spirituality. This is not lessening the power of faith and prayer but enhancing it!

In the Old Testament, after the miraculous healing took place as the children of Israel began their journey, God gave them laws of what they could eat and what they could not eat. This was not to punish them but to keep them healthy. He gave them the manna in the desert. This was probably because He could not trust their appetites, and eating according to their appetites would bring sickness so He fed them manna and health was theirs all of the years that they traveled. However, God allowed then to die in the wilderness and they were not allowed to go into the promised land because of their disobedience.

As we partake in the ceremony of the Lord's Table, we are to examine ourselves to see if we are partaking unworthily (without faith and obedience). Are we obeying His commandments? Are we discerning each other with the same value as ourselves? Are we obeying His commands to love one another? (He wants us to be healthy in our souls - our mind, will, emotions) By the same degree that we are obedient in discerning the body (the spiritual body - the church) and the physical body of Christ (the sacrifice he made), I believe we can expect health to be in our churches and individual members. Our physical health will be apparent in the wake of our spiritual health. As we began to take responsibility for our own health and understand the fuel our body needs to repair itself and to keep us healthy depends largely on the foods we put into our mouths, we will be working with the Holy Spirit and doing our part to fight sickness. Sickness will lose its power over our bodies just as sin loses it power over our spirits. We will be as free from sickness as we are from sin. Jesus bore them both for us. And He wore the crown of thorns to provide for healing of the mind and emotions. Jesus has provided healing in these areas of our lives. Receive them by faith, began to walk in this knowledge so that His bearing them will not be in vain!

I know and understand that it is appointed unto us to die. This is the door way from this world to the place we call heaven. This is the ultimate healing. I believe we receive healing from God in many different ways. I am not against the use of the medical world in assisting in our healing. Faith in God can and does compliment the work of the doctors. Healing comes only from God and He has made our bodies wonderful and with abilities to heal itself but it needs the proper nutrition. Many things the medical world has to offer in the way of surgery, medicines, therapy, etc., will aid in our comforts...., but healing comes from within and from God. Wrong attitudes can bring about emotions that can cause physical illness. Sometimes we need deliverance from underlying fears, resentments, self-centeredness and guilt. These deliverances are avenues of healing. I believe that we can have quality life here as we journey in this world and it is according to our faith and obedience as we put into practice the Word of God. God's word will change our physical bodies when it is believed and acted upon, but what we feel will never change God's Word..

I don't expect to live forever but if I am alive, I WANT TO LIVE!

Nutrition for the Spirit Man

A person needs a diet of special nutrients in order to remain healthy. It is suggested by nutritionists that if the cells in our bodies receive these nutrients, it is impossible for disease to live in our bodies. **Disease (even cancer) begins with a single cell,** and in a healthy, well nourished body the healthy cells (referred to as our immune system) destroy the diseased cells thus stopping the spread of that disease. Diet is what we eat. Nutrition is that which the cells actually get.

The spirit man also needs a special diet. Let us compare the two. Let's look at first the natural, then the spiritual.

PROTEIN

Protein comes from a Greek word meaning, "of first importance" and is one of the most important elements for maintenance of good health and vitality and is of primary importance in the growth and development of all body tissues. It is the major source of building material for muscles, blood, skin, hair, nails and internal organs, including the heart and the brain. As well as being the major source of building material for the body, protein is also a source of heat and energy.

Even though protein is of utmost importance, it is also the most difficult to digest. The proteins that we eat cannot be used by the body as nutrition for our cells. Rather, dietary protein is broken down into its constituent **amino acids** which the body then uses to build the specific protein it needs. Thus it is the amino acids rather than protein that are the essential nutrients. This is accomplished with the help of enzymes.

Our spiritual protein is the Word of God.

We need a daily diet of the Word of God. As we feed on the word, we will become strong Christians. We will learn how to please The Father. We will grow healthy to maturity and will be able to endure difficulties. We will be proven; thus producing faithfulness and the ability to accept responsibilities that He gives to us.

"For though by this time you ought to be teachers, you have need again for someone to teach you the elementary principles of the oracles of God, and you have come to need milk and not solid food. For everyone who partakes only of milk is not accustomed to the word of righteousness for he is a babe. But solid food is for the mature who because of practice have their senses trained to discern good and evil." Hebrews 5:12-14

ENZYMES

Enzymes are specific protein molecules that initiate or speed chemical reactions in the body. Enzymes carry the nutrition to parts of the body and are essential for digesting food, for stimulating the brain, for providing cellular energy and for repairing all tissues, organs, and cells. Life as we know it could not exist without the action of enzymes. Digestion is the process of breaking complex substances (protein) into more simple substances which the body can use **(amino acids)**, either as tissue building/repair or energy. If digestion does not occur, then neither does nutrition, the food we eat will not be circulated into our cells to benefit our body. "Live" foods contain enzymes, food that has not been cooked or processed. (fruit, vegetables, nuts, seeds, ECT.)

ENZYMES FOR THE SPIRIT MAN ARE PRAYER and MEDITATION

This is when personal revelation of the Word happens. We cannot understand the Word of God without time spent in prayer and meditation. We need to let the Word of God "roll around on the inside of us." When our spiritual digestive system is not functioning, we can be fed a good protein diet of the Word and still appear unfed, malnourished, and stunted in growth. Without digestion the Word never becomes assimilated and never gets into our circulatory system where our spirit man is nourished. As a result, we do not have the energy or desire to practice the Word and therefore a changed nature is not produced. Many have sat in church for years and have received good teaching and are seemingly unaffected; not experiencing Christian growth or a changed nature. When problems arise, there is no strength or stability. The food was there but the lack of a personal prayer life, meditation and practice of the Word hindered the growing process.

"Now we have received, not the spirit of the world, but the Spirit who is from God, that we might know the things freely given to us by God which things we also speak, not in words taught by human wisdom, but those taught by the Spirit, combining spiritual thoughts with spiritual words. But a natural man does not accept the things of God; for they are foolishness to him and he cannot understand them, because they are spiritually appraised. But he who is spiritual appraises all things, yet he himself is appraised by no man. For who has known the mind of the Lord, that He should instruct Him? But we have the mind of Christ." 1 Cor. 2:13-16

LIPIDS

Lipids are the oils (dietary fat) in our body. Oil is needed, especially during infancy and childhood for normal brain development; and throughout life is essential to provide energy and support growth. Oil is also needed in our diet to keep our cells soft and pliable in order to take in nourishment and also to eliminate waste. Lipids are a must for a healthy body! There are two different kinds of fats or oil in our diets: saturated and unsaturated. Saturated fatty acids are found primarily in animal products. An excessive high intake of saturated fats in our diets have been linked to many of the degenerative diseases which we face today. Unsaturated fatty acids are found in certain nuts, seeds and vegetables. Our diets should lean toward the unsaturated fatty acids for maximum health.

THE LIPID NEEDED BY OUR SPIRIT MAN IS THE "OIL" OF THE HOLY SPIRIT

With the Holy Spirit controlling our life, we will be sensitive to the needs of the Spirit and yielded to His activity and direction in our lives. Without the Spirit control, we will become hardened and given to our own pleasures and desires. With the Holy Spirit censoring our thought life, we are also able to let the "stuff" in our lives pass on by as waste and not allow it to indwell us or become a part of our natures. We have been born again and we are new creations in Christ. The Holy Spirit will guide us in the process of becoming partakers of His divine nature. The Holy Spirit is not an option for a Christian …it is a must!

I compare the spiritual difference between the saturated and un-saturated fatty acids to "relationship" versus "religion". If we are maintaining a relationship with the Lord Jesus through the Holy Spirit anointing, we are taking in unsaturated nutrition. Our spirit is being fed. If we are trying to obey man inspired laws of doctrine or religion, our path way to the Holy Spirit will become clogged and it will be very difficult to maintain a relationship with the Lord and receive direction through the Holy Spirit. Religion is food for the natural or carnal nature of man and will not satisfy the spirit. Spiritual "degenerative diseases" will begin to be manifested and spiritual death is inevitable if a person does not deviate from this path.

"For the mind set on the flesh (old nature) is death, but the mind set on the Spirit is life and peace, because the mind set on the flesh is hostile toward God; for it does not subject itself to the law of God, for it is not able to do so; and those who are in the flesh cannot please God". Rom. 8:6-8

"But the Helper, the Holy Spirit, whom the Father will send in my name, He will teach you all things and bring to your remembrance all that I said to you. " St. John 14:26

"Now we have received, not the spirit of the world, but the Spirit who is from God, that we might know the things freely given to us by God, which things we also speak, not in words taught by human wisdom,

but in those taught by the Spirit, combining spiritual thoughts with spiritual words." 1 Cor 2:12

"That He would grant you, according to the riches of His glory, to be strengthened with power through His Spirit in the inner man, so that Christ may dwell in your hearts through faith, and that you being rooted and grounded in love may be able to comprehend with all the saints what is the breadth and length and height and depth and to know the love of Christ which surpasses knowledge that you may be filled up to all the fullness of God." Eph. 3:16-19

"But when He, the Spirit of truth, comes, He will guide you into all the truth; for He will not speak on His own initiative, but whatever He hears, He will speak and He will disclose to you what is to come." St. John 16:13

CARBOHYDRATES

Carbohydrates are our chief source of energy for all body functions and muscular exertion, and are necessary to assist in the digestion and assimilation of other foods. Good carbohydrates are those found in honey, fruits, vegetables and whole grains. Carbohydrate snacks containing saturated fats, sugars and starches provide the body with almost instant energy by causing a sudden rise in the blood sugar level. However when the blood sugar level drops again rapidly, it causes a feeling of fatigue, dizziness, nervousness, headache and a craving for more sweet food. This produces a nature that is moody and changeable. An over indulgence in starchy, saturated fat and sweet foods may crowd out other essential foods from the diet and can therefore result in nutritional deficiency as well as obesity. Diets high in refined carbohydrates are usually low in other nutrients. A craving for "sweets" is a signal that we are lacking in other nutrients. Research has connected degenerative diseases such as diabetes, heart disease, high blood pressure, anemia, kidney disorders and cancer to an over abundance of refined carbohydrate food in our diet.

I COMPARE OUR SPIRIT MAN CARBOHYDRATES TO OUR SOULISH EXPERIENCES-OUR 5 SENSES..THOSE THINGS WE SEE, FEEL, HEAR, THINK ABOUT, OUR EMOTIONS.

Our soul/senses have been programmed by our experiences in the world and when we come to Christ, our soul/senses must be renewed. "The Lord is my shepherd,...he restores my soul" Psa. 23! We must feed our spirit man a blast of restorative, renewal "carbs" which will produce energy! As we begin to read the Word of God and put it into practice, as we begin to desire to do those things which please the Lord, as we yield our thoughts, desires, and behavior to the control of the Holy Spirit, our natures begin to change and line up with His will for us. A mature Christian will be in control of His emotions and have charge over his behavior. Others will begin to see the manifestations of the fruit of the Spirit in our nature (behavior) which is: love, joy, peace, patience, kindness, goodness, faithfulness, gentleness and self control. This does not happen at once, but is a process. If we do not deal with our soulish appetites and we remain in carnality, we will never mature spiritually but will live on soulish experiences based on our five senses (emotions). We will have a roller coaster Christian experience. Even, going from church to church never becoming stable, never becoming responsible but looking for "sugar coated" ministry that will satisfy the soulish hunger. A "refined carbohydrate" Christian is controlled by his emotions. Many times, it is not our actions that reveal where we are in our Christian walk and growth, but it is our re-actions or responses to difficult situations that tell on us. A child in the natural will reach for a candy in preference to a carrot if given a choice. A carnal Christian is the same. This person is looking for the taste he likes, rather than nutrition for health. He is more contented with fast food, (quick fixes) and is not disciplined in the Word or his prayer life.

Now the works of the flesh are evident: immorality, impurity, sensuality, idolatry, sorcery, enmities, strife, jealousy, outburst of anger, disputes, dissensions, factions, envying, drunkenness, carousing, and things like these....those who practice these things will not inherit the kingdom of God.

"For the time will come when they will not endure sound doctrine; but wanting to have their ears tickled, they will accumulate for themselves teachers in accordance to their own desires; and will turn away their ears from the truth and will turn aside to myths". 11 Timothy 4:2-3

"In reference to your former manner of life, you lay aside the old self, which is being corrupted in accordance with the lusts of deceit, and that you be renewed in the spirit of your mind, and put on the new self, which in the likeness of God has been created in righteousness and holiness of the truth." Ephesians 4:22-24

"And do not be conformed to this world but be transformed by the renewing of your mind that you may prove what the will of God is, that which is good and acceptable and perfect." Romans 12:2

VITAMINS AND MINERALS

Vitamins and Minerals build and repair body structures and help fight disease or infection. Vitamins and minerals assist in regulating metabolism or energy. They are constituents of the bones, teeth, soft tissue, muscle, blood and nerve cells. They maintain physiological processes, helping to strengthen skeletal structures and preserve the vigor of the heart and brain as well as muscle and nerve systems.

OUR SPIRIT MAN VITAMINS AND MINERALS ARE OUR FELLOWSHIP, OUR PRAISE AND WORSHIP

When we receive an injury or we are confronted with the beginnings of a sin or a discouragement (from any source), usually, the first thing that happens....we just don't feel like going to church and we begin to distance ourselves from our church body. We need to stay in the church-body where God has placed us. **Remember that disease begins with a single cell and sin can begin with a single thought!** Stay in the body! Continue in fellowship! Allow the rest of the body to minister to you and destroy the diseased cell. There are times of healing in our praise and worship. Our spiritual immune system can "zone in" on the problem and correct it before it can become a full blown major problem to deal with. I have received major revelations for my life during worship time. There is healing in fellowship. Without this ministry one to the other, disease (sin) will overcome us and death is sure. Being a part of a church body is God's idea, not man's idea!

"And they were continually devoting themselves to the apostles teaching and to fellowship, to the breaking of bread and to prayer." Acts 2:42

"Let us consider how to stimulate one another to love and good deeds, not forsaking our own assembling together, as is the habit of some, but encouraging one another and all the more as you see the day drawing near." Hebrews 10:24

WATER

Water is not only the most abundant nutrient found in the body; it also is by far the most important nutrient. It is responsible for and involved in nearly every body process, including digestion, absorption, circulation and excretion. Water is the primary transporter of nutrients throughout the body and is necessary for all building functions in the body. Water helps maintain a normal body temperature and is essential for carrying waste material out of the body. Water helps to maintain proper muscle tone and prevents dehydration. When our body gets the water it needs to function, its fluids are perfectly balanced and natural thirst returns. The less water you drink, the less you want to drink! We need to develop a desire for water.

I COMPARE WATER FOR THE SPIRIT MAN WITH THE ANOINTING

The word Christ means "the anointed one". The anointing is the element that enables us to partake of the realm of the Spiritual. When we are anointed; or in the atmosphere of the anointing, we hear with His understanding (because we have the mind of Christ). The quality of our physical life is directly related to the care and food that it has received. So also, that which we are in our spirit man must be nourished and built up. If we receive the word of God only with our minds, our spirit man is not being fed. For the ministry of the Word to become spiritual food, it must be anointed. It must come from the presence of the Lord through an anointed ministry in an atmosphere of the anointing. There must be an openness of heart and receptivity of spirit in order to receive. John 3:6 "that which is born of flesh is flesh and that which is born of Spirit is Spirit". The Lord patiently waits for His Body to grow and mature. Let us eat of the food that enables us to grow and drink plenty of His anointing-water. If you do not have a spiritual desire for the things of the spirit, just begin to drink... the more you drink and eat of the Spirit, the more you will hunger and thirst for His righteousness.

"He who believes in me as the Scripture said, From his innermost being shall flow rivers of living water"
John 7:38

EXERCISE FOR HEALTH!

Apart from nutrition, one more item is necessary for a healthy body and this is EXERCISE. We are told that regular exercise improves digestion and elimination, increases endurance and energy levels, reduces stress and anxiety. We should never become sedentary. We should continue to keep moving and being active in order to maintain health.

THE SPRIT MAN'S EXERCISE IS PRACTICING THE WORD OF GOD

James tells us to be "doers of the word and not hearers only". We are changed from glory to glory as we PRACTICE the word of God. We must CHOOSE to practice the nature of God! 1st Peter chapter one tells us that we become partakers of His divine nature by practicing the word of God. It is up to us to put new thoughts and directions in control and we have the Holy Spirit to help us do that. We yield our senses (mind, will and emotions) to the Holy Spirit's control. We obey his commandments not because we feel like doing it but because it is His will for our lives. We love and forgive others, not according to our feelings but because we have made the choice to do it, and our feelings will (in time) line up with the Word. It is His will that we love and forgive...even when it is hard to do.

Practice the word of God until it becomes a part of our nature. That is how habits are formed and that is how we will become changed! It will be awkward and unnatural to "put aside the old nature" and "be transformed by the renewing of our minds" but it can happen.

He didn't give us commandments to appease our five senses, but to change us. We will not always feel like obeying Him. Habits are formed as we continue to practice his word. His word will become a part of our nature. For example, when a baby first begins to feed himself, he is pretty messy and yet, with practice he can handle that job pretty good! It has become a part of his nature. When one starts learning to play an instrument, it is very awkward and the sounds are anything but harmonious, however, eventually, he can put his fingers in the correct places and make beautiful music...it has become a part of his nature! We will "do" his will because it has become a part of our nature.

We become strengthened in our Christian walk because we PRACTICE His will. We do not have to live void of feeling, but our feelings must line up with the Word of God. As we practice His word our nature will change. It is God's action and interference in our lives that is designed to bring us to the desired relationship with Him.. There are some things that we are required to "lay aside", Ephesians 4:22-32 "lay aside your old self and be renewed in the spirit of your mind....and put on your new self which is in the likeness of God. Here are some things we are to "lay aside":

Bitterness - harsh, long term disagreement

Wrath - reaction to bitterness

Anger - sudden anger, temper

Clamor - demands, arguing

Slander - damages another's influence

Malice - active ill will

God's desire is to take all that we are and mold us into His image, keeping the good and eliminating all that He cannot use. The ultimate purpose of God is to change us into His nature and to reveal His power through His people!

This Christ-like behavior is not a magical-mystical thing that "zaps" us and one morning we are suddenly different. It is a process! When we are born again, God's Spirit is united with our spirits and a new creation is born of an incorruptible seed (sperm). 1st Peter 1:2:This involves our spirits through faith and is not based on our feelings-our five senses. I have heard my husband say that God's Spirit becomes our "battering ram," knocking down strong holds in our natures and allowing the new nature to have control. Our desires, thought patterns, and ambitions begin to change as we yield to the Spirit of God who indwells us.

However, being filled with the Holy Spirit involves our emotions (five senses) and is an experience. "You will receive power after the Holy Spirit is come upon you." Acts 1:8: The first concern that we need power over is our own self, our choices, wills and emotions. Our old nature has been programmed by the principles of the world depending on our education, social status, environment, self concept, etc. All of the desires and controls of the old nature are still a part of us in our thoughts and our behavior. God desires to take us and change us into a person for His use and purpose. It is a process!

"Let no one deceive you, the one who PRACTICES righteousness is righteous and he who PRACTICES sin is of the devil...." 1 John 3:7

In 2nd Peter chapter one, he gives a lot of things to think about, to add to our exercise program and in verse 10, he states, " *as long as you PRACTICE these things, you will never stumble, for in this way the entrance into the eternal kingdom of our Lord and Savior Jesus Christ will be abundantly supplied to you*".

Have you ever been at the right place and the right time to be used of God? You have spoken into a person's life when they desperately needed attention from God. There is nothing that satisfies the appetite of the spirit man more than doing the will of God. I am reminded of Jesus at the well. He had sent His disciples to buy food. While they were gone, Jesus ministered to the woman at the well. When the disciples returned, Jesus was not hungry. He said that He had food that they knew not of! Once you have tasted this in your life, your spirit man will hunger for this taste again and again. **Jesus said that His food was to do the will of His Father!**

"Let the one who does wrong, still do wrong...the one who is filthy, still be filthy, let the one who is righteous still practice righteousness... let the one who is holy still keep himself holy...verse 12...behold I am coming quickly...." We will not be able to change when Jesus returns. **Whatever we are practicing, that is the way we will stand before Him.**

A well balanced nutritious diet; and an exercise program will cause the spirit man to excel and produce a fruitful ministry in faithfulness and responsibility. The fruit of the Spirit will be manifested in our behavior. These are character traits of God and are formed in us by degrees and under pressure (it is a process) as we abide in Christ, our character is transformed to be like the most lovely character of Jesus.

THE END

RELATIONSHIPS
LETS TALK ABOUT MEN AND WOMEN

The church and marriage are two institutions not only ordained by God but invented by Him. Satan's job is to kill, steal and destroy God's plans for us. Satan is out to destroy our homes; if he can destroy homes, he can weaken the church. The church is made up of husbands, wives, families. If he can weaken the family, he can weaken the church. When the battle rages, whether we choose to go into open warfare (ending in divorce) or a silent war, the results are the same: less effectiveness in the work of the Lord and in our lives. We will never be on a higher level of spirituality than we are in our homes. What or who we are at home is what or who we are!

The PERFECT (MATURE) POWERFUL CHURCH that Christ is coming after begins in our homes! There were problems in the churches of the New Testament and there are still problems in our churches and homes today.

Paul told the Galatian Church, "*if you bite and devour one another, you will be consumed by one another*".

Concerning the Corinthian Church, Paul stated that divisions exist... strife, angry tempers, disputes...".

Paul wrote to the Ephesian Church, "*let no unwholesome word proceed from your mouth, do not grieve the Holy Spirit of God...let all bitterness (sharp, harsh, disagreeable, resentful, cynical) and wrath (reaction to bitterness) and anger (temper-anger) and clamor (demand or complaint) and slander (an utterance that damages another's reputation) be put away from you with all malice (active ill will). Be kind to one another, tender-hearted, forgiving each other just as God in Christ has forgiven you.*

Never-the-less, God is still at work in us causing us to desire to do those things that please Him and He is still coming after that perfect (mature), powerful church...made up of families!

I want to share here some notes taken from a Bible study:

The name Adam means, *man, human being.* Adam represents all of us. What God intended for Adam, He intended for the entire human race. God gave Adam, Eve and their descendants dominion over the entire earth and all creation. We see this in Genesis 1:26-28. We also see this in Psalm 8:3, *"Adam" was* God's re-presenter on earth. In Verse 6 he was to *"rule".* Adam was God's manager over the earth. He was God's mediator, go-between or representative.

Adam was created in God's image. God did not give away ownership of the earth, but He did assign the responsibility of governing it to humanity! He gave us dominion over the entire earth and all creation.

What does it mean to represent someone? To present again,..to re-present. WE ARE TO RE-PRESENT GOD ON THE EARTH! (Dictionary: to exhibit the image and counterpart of; to speak and act with authority on the part of; to be a substitute or agent for).

God made Adam, the human, so much the same as himself that it was illusionary. God created man in His own image...in the image of God He created him: male and female, he created them.

The Hebrew word of image is shadow, a phantom or an illusion. An illusion is something you think you see, but on closer observation you discover your eyes have tricked you....for a moment I thought it was God, but it's only Adam. Adam was very much like God! God even gave us the ability to create eternal spirits, something he had entrusted to no other creature; not only that but, humanity was crowned with God's own glory! Glory: heavy, weighty, concept of authority. Adam represented God with full authority. Adam was in charge! Glory also has reference to the nature and character of God. When creation looked at Adam, they were supposed to see God, and they did, until Adam sinned and fell short of the glory (NATURE AND CHARACTER) of God.

GOD IS NO LONGER RECOGNIZED IN FALLEN HUMANKIND.

PLEASE THINK ABOUT THIS...IF THE EARTH REMAINED A PARADISE, IT WOULD BE BECAUSE OF HUMANKIND. THINGS BECAME MESSED UP BECAUSE OF HUMANKIND! HUMANITY REALLY WAS AND IS IN CHARGE!

Psalm 8:6: *"Thou has made him to rule over the works of thy hands. Thou has put all things under his feet"*

LET'S START FROM THE BEGINNING

"God said Let us make man in our image and our likeness...and God created man in His own image, in the image of God He created him: male and female He created them" (Gen 1:26 & 27).

Gen 2:7,8: *"Then the Lord God formed man from dust from the ground and breathed into his nostrils the breath of life and man became a living being."*

Man was created in God's image...and God has both male and female attributes.

Psalms 147:2-5: *The Lord builds up Jerusalem: He gathers the outcast of Israel, he heals the broken hearted and binds up their wounds. He counts the number of the stars; He gives names to all of them. Great is our Lord and abundant in strength; His understanding is infinite."*

Female attributes = nurturing qualities
Male attributes = math abilities, science, strength
Joshua 5 - Captain of the Lord of host (Leads into battles)

WE DO NOT KNOW HOW LONG ADAM WAS IN THE GARDEN ALONE but there came a time when God looked at him and said, *"It isn't good for him to be alone, I will make him a helper".*

"So the Lord caused a deep sleep to fall upon the man and he slept; and he took one of the ribs and closed up the flesh in that place. Vs 22

and the Lord God fashioned into a woman the rib which he had taken from the man and brought her to the man Vs23 and the man said "this is bone of my bone and flesh of my flesh" (Gen 2:21).

Perhaps more than only a rib was taken from him...but the female attributes were removed and given to the woman. When she was brought to the man, he knew her as part of himself.

HAVE YOU EVER NOTICED THAT MEN AND WOMEN ARE TOTALLY DIFFERENT?

We are different not only physically but emotionally and mentally. Our brains actually process information differently.

Gary Smally, a Christian psychologist, explains: from 6-8 weeks into pregnancy, a chemical is released into the womb called testosterone. It bypasses the female baby and washes out half of the pathways between the right and left brain of the male baby.

MEN function predominately from the left side. Gary Smally says that men are not much on talk; however, I think that depends on the subject! If the subject is sports, hunting, fishing, motorized vehicles, building, occupations, vacations, they do pretty good! It is mostly dealing with feelings and relationships that they have problems talking about! What do you think?

Women are more comfortable with talk. Gary Smally says women speak about 25,000 words and men speak about 12,000 words daily. He gave an example of four year old girls and boys who were monitored. The girls were verbal, playing with imaginary friends, etc., the boys mostly just made noise and sounds.

MEN SEE THE VISIBLE, DEAL WITH FACTS AND LOGIC, EASILY FOCUS ON ONE THING, FOCUS ON PHYSICAL SURROUNDINGS (ON GOALS, PRODUCTIVITY, HOBBIES). THEY HAVE A MORE NARROW POINT OF VIEW, GOAL ORIENTED AND NOT EASY TO "GET IN TOUCH" WITH THEIR FEELINGS, HARD FOR MEN TO EXPRESS THEIR FEELINGS. IT TAKES EFFORT TO CROSS THE PATHWAY TO FEELINGS (right side). THIS ENABLES MEN TO HUNT, GO TO WAR, TO BE WOMEN'S PROTECTION. GOD MADE THEM THIS WAY.

There is a lot about men that I do not understand! There are words of a county/western song talking about the difference in men and women: "She sees Bambi and I see antlers on my wall!" I would have a hard time shooting little Bambi off the trail but most men would not!

Recently, we were at a lake with my brother, Perry, and his wife. They like to fish. I take a book to read and I enjoy a boat ride.

Anyway, it was cold and the men would get up at 5:00 AM even while it was sleeting cold rain to go out and "conquer" those fish. I rolled over and looked at my husband and said, "You are so silly."

Later in the morning, we were all together and having breakfast. My brother was talking about how it was so cold and he was shaking so hard and he could hardly bait his hook. I said, "I do not understand why you think you have to go out there when it is so cold and miserable." He said, "Well, Sis, that is what men do; we are hunters and gatherers." I told him, "Well, I am, too, but I go to a mall". :^)

A MAN CHECKS THE HEADLINES. A WOMAN READS THE FINE PRINT, DETAILS! WE ARE DIFFERENT!

WOMAN: More talkative; many pathways between right/left sides; in touch with feelings and emotions and VERY ABLE TO EXPRESS THEM. Women can change steps in mid-stride; do several things at the same time; sense the invisible; more open to the spirit world; and pick up on the slightest change in relationships.

A woman is more prone to change her mind. A woman's brain comes into contact with more information but generally has greater difficulty in making a decision, bouncing pros and cons back and forth, utilizing both hemispheres, dealing with feelings and emotions.

A MAN IS NOT SO EASILY SWAYED and is more focused because with less information it is easier to make a decision, but he is subject to his own narrow world sometimes ruled by his ego.

MEN GET BORED WITH "*TALKING IT OUT*" BUT WOMEN ARE ENERGIZED! That's why women need other women, good friends to talk to!

Women feel frustrated at men for their lack of understanding and refusal to communicate. I tell my husband if I were a computer, he'd have me figured out by now and would be able to push all my right buttons at the appropriate times!

Men get frustrated at us and accuse us of changing our minds and nagging ...as communication degenerates, men make accusations and women issue ultimatums. (or visa versa)
EVERYONE LOSES.

THERE IS NO INFERIORITY ON EITHER PART INSINUATED IN GOD'S PERFECT CREATION. ALL THINGS ARE FAIR, EQUAL AND BALANCED, YET WE FULFILL DIFFERENT PURPOSES: THE TWO SEXES EXERCISE POWER DIFFERENTLY.

MAN - POWER OF AUTHORITY
WOMAN - POWER OF INFLUENCE

GOD MADE A HELPER FOR ADAM!!

A helper is not of less importance! Compare Ps 54:4: *God is our helper.*

John 14:26: *The Holy Spirit is our helper, comforter, intercessor counselor, advocate (One who is in support of something).*

THE PURPOSE OF A WOMAN IS A HELPER AND IS TO EXERCISE INFLUENCE.

WOMEN HAVE BEEN GIVEN A TREMENDOUS POWER OF PERSUASION!

Women can use their power of influence for good or evil, to build up or tear down. We are masters at manipulation!

The feminist movement today is doing great evil because the devil is using the strength/power of women's emotions to do his bidding. Satan counterfeits every good thing in an attempt to make us stumble into his kingdom, and in his kingdom is envy, strife, selfish ambition, confusion and every evil thing. There are no absolutes, no right/ wrongs and no discipline. The feminist movement began with the effort to establish equality for women in the work place. However, there has always been equality in God's eyes, even though we are different and were created for different purposes.

MEN AND WOMEN HAVE BECOME FRUSTRATED WITH EACH OTHER BECAUSE WE DO NOT APPRECIATE AND EMBRACE OUR UNIQUE DIFFERENCES AND PURPOSES.

Proverbs 12:4 says that an excellent wife is a crown to her husband

Strong's concordance: CROWN - to encircle for attack or protection. A woman of God is to encompass him against attacks and for protection. Man usually focuses on one thing and often does not see traps or pitfalls that Satan has placed in front of him.

Psalms 5:12 says that God blesses us and CROWNS (surrounds) us with favor.

Have we used our position to attack or for protection, loving kindness, compassion, favor?

Another definition for HELPER is a corresponding part.

BY SEPARATING THE POWERS, God could express himself more fully with a greater range of function.

TO WOMEN GOD HAS GIVEN POWER OF INFLUENCE AND TO MEN POWER OF AUTHORITY.

HOWEVER, GOD HAS EMPHASIZED HIS CHARACTERISTIC IN WOMEN THAT INVOLVES HIS HEART, EMOTIONS, SENSITIVITY, FEELINGS, UNDERSTANDING, COMPASSION! OUR HOMES NEED WIVES AND MOTHERS IN THEM AND NOT EQUAL HEADS!

TWO HEADS IS A FREAK!

A couple only will enjoy the full benefits of marriage if they embrace their mates as their perfectly designed complement. Many men are too insecure to depend upon or acknowledge the advice of their wives. It seems to threaten their sense of leadership. However, a woman will trust, admire and willingly support a man who will listen to and consider her advice. Developing a relationship of interdependence strengthens, not weakens a husband's proper position in marriage.

There are too many exposed areas in which a man without a wife's protection can be attacked and defeated, both naturally and spiritually. A husband who does not recognize the gift of his wife is opening himself to being deceived by his own pride and ambition.

The bible tells us to submit to one another in the fear of Christ. My husband told me that "submit" is not a dirty word. It actually means to combine our resources for a common goal.

WOMEN, we can help our mates in learning how to share his heart and get in touch with his feelings.

Women have intuitions (a gift from God). Women pick up on things in the spirit realm and sense needs of others.

THE FIRST TIME OUR POWER OF INFLUENCE WAS USED was in the garden. Eve was susceptible to the serpent's enticing words and his power strategy, *"You will be like God."* Humanism is not new. Eve fell while living in Paradise! Satan is still using the same tactics today! He is approaching women and causing women to be dissatisfied with God's plans for their lives and uses the strength of their emotions to do his bidding!

EVE MADE THE DECISION ON HER OWN WITHOUT THE COUNSEL OF ADAM OR GOD!

A WOMAN'S MIND/FEELINGS ARE UNLOCKED WITH WORDS. Words are spiritual containers that unlock her emotions and feelings.

Eve was deceived with words—a power strategy. Humanism is not new, it began in the garden.

A woman is moved by what she hears! WORDS ARE POWERFUL! Man was created in God's image and He spoke the world into existence. Words are creative. Relationships are created or killed with words.

Example: An abused woman will stay with a man who abuses her because afterwards he will say he is sorry and that he loves her, promises to never do it again and she listens to his words rather than what he has done to her.

IN MATTHEW FIVE, JESUS IS DEALING WITH RELATIONSHIPS and speaks against murder, being angry with each other, name calling (raca, you fool). He knew that words can kill!

Proverbs 25:11: *Words rightly spoken are like apples of gold in settings of silver.* Words are valuable!

To a woman silence is neglect! To withhold verbal appreciation/ praise from a woman will cause her to develop a feeling of unworthiness, low self esteem, insecurities, fears and a lack of confidence in herself. A woman has a tendency to believe what she is told.

A WOMAN CAN BE INFLUENCED BY A SMOOTH TALKING MAN!

A WOMAN'S POWER OF INFLUENCE IS VITAL TO A MAN AND A MAN'S POWER OF AUTHORITY IS VITAL TO A WOMAN. We develop a trust in each other. We can bring about God's perfect will when we work together to build up each other's strengths. The anointed, Christ centered wife who is growing spiritually, giving attention, love and ministry to her husband will find her love and support for him greatly affects his inner spiritual growth. A WOMAN HAS A GOD GIVEN DESIRE AND CAPACITY TO GIVE REVERENCE AND RESPECT AND A MAN NEEDS THIS.

Someone once said the moral state of the nations depends on the spiritual state of the women. The hand that rocks the cradle is the hand that rules the world!

A MAN IS ATTRACTED/INFLUENCED WITH HIS EYES, what he sees! His mind/feelings are unlocked by images.

When a man SEES a woman who is Christ centered, living out God's word, being changed from glory to glory, this can motivate him more that the words she speaks (the preaching and nagging).

When a man is attracted to a godly woman she can influence him into a spiritual purity that will have a cleansing affect on his life. When a man is attracted to a worldly woman whose moral values are worldly or sexually perverse, she can lead him into sin and degrading passions.

WOMEN! WE HAVE THE POWER OF INFLUENCE, WE CAN BUILD GOD CONFIDENCE IN OUR **HUSBANDS!**

A woman's power is tremendous in scope and importance and we have used it for such poor purposes. We can lift an eyebrow, pucker lips, give out a squeak, which are gestures that translate into power! Man has been known to walk across burning sand on a beach due to a flirtatious look from a bikini clad female—THAT'S POWER! MEN ARE MOVED BY WHAT THEY SEE!

Relationship barometers: Things that will satisfy a man will not satisfy a woman because men and women are different:

MEN- sexual fulfillment
    admiration and respect
WOMEN-level of communication/verbal
    appreciation and security

The lyrics of one country song goes like this, "Let's have a little less talk and a lot more action" (written by man! :^)

WISDOM IN ACTION:

Eph 5:33: let the wife see that she shows respect and reverence to her husband

Eph 5:25,28: husbands love your wives as Christ loved the Church/. Husbands love your wives as your own body ... (You know, you are always on your mind)

TO DO LIST: Women: notice, regard, honor, prefer, venerate (look upon him with feelings of deep respect) defer (yield with courtesy) praise and admire him.

Men: do the same but do not forget to say the words!

Proverbs 25:11: words rightly spoken are like apples of gold in a setting of silver . WORDS ARE VALUABLE!

A PRUDENT WIFE IS FROM THE LORD Proverbs 19:14:

Prudent means to be wise, understanding and circumspect. She is attentive to everything and watches in all directions to guard against error or danger, even in the unseen world.

WHEN A MAN HAS THE INFLUENCE OF A PRUDENT WIFE, THE LORD GIVES HIM FAVOR. Proverbs 18:22

A WOMAN WHO SEARCHES FOR AND EMBRACES WISDOM MAY KNOW THINGS BEFORE THEY HAPPEN— "WOMAN'S INTUITION." THIS IS PART OF HER PURPOSE AND AN AVENUE OF HER POWER.

SATAN WOULD LIKE TO SHORT CIRCUIT THE POWER OF GOD IN YOUR LIFE AND THE FIRST METHOD HE WOULD USE WOULD BE TO GET YOU OUT OF POSITION!

Sometimes getting into our position involves daily attitude adjustments. For an example I refer to my submission to my husband as my **"as unto ministry"**.

Yes, there are times my feelings and emotions do not want to "go along" with whatever he has decided. I may not even "like' him at the moment. That is when I "submit as unto the Lord". Remember: "submit" is not a dirty word. It means to rally our resources for a common goal!

Eph 5:22: *"Wives, submit to your own husbands as unto the Lord."*

Submitting to God through another shows a greater degree of faith than submitting to God directly. REMINDER: God-Christ-Man-Woman (Eph 5:23)

God created woman for a specific purpose and the most powerful place she can be is in a position to accomplish that purpose. The power (anointing) of God is released when we are in our position, whether we are in authority or influence. Be subject to one another out of reverence of Christ.

When a person feels oppressed by the call to submit, something is out of order (bullying?) I don't know of a woman who would not lovingly and willingly submit to the man who loved her as Christ loved the church or as he loved his own self!

The power of authority is released when the one in position of authority makes godly decisions.

The power of influence is released when one displays a willingness to submit to those decisions. There are times that a wrong decision will be made, but because we are submitted to God, He will not leave us in error. He will continue to lead us into a correction and we will continue serving Him together.

CHRISTIANS ARE CALLED OUT FROM DOING THINGS THE WAY THE WORLD DOES THEM.

JESUS'S SUBMISSION TO THE CROSS BROKE THE POWER OF THE DEVIL OVER US FOR ALL ETERNITY!

Men and women exercise both authority and submission at different times and different ways. Example: in the work place a woman may have a place of authority, however, at home she is still in subjection to the authority of her husband. A woman has authority over her children. A man submits in the work place to women with authority or to a choir director and etc. We are primarily speaking and addressing relationships between husbands and wives.

We are a part of that mighty, powerful, mature church that will be marching across the land doing the works of God. We will be mighty by doing it God's way.

THE SPIRIT REALM OPENS TO US WHEN WE ARE IN SUBMISSION TO GOD AND WE ALIGN OURSELVES WITH CHRIST AND RELEASE GOD'S POWER AND ANOINTING INTO OUR LIVES.

GOD DEALT WITH ME IN A VERY DEFINITE WAY CONCERNING SUBMISSION. I HAVE NOT ALWAYS BEEN AS SUBMISSIVE AS I AM TODAY. LEON HAS NOT ALWAYS BEEN THE EXCELLENT HUSBAND AND LEADER THAT HE IS TODAY. IT TAKES SOME DYING TO SELF AND BEING WILLING TO SUBMIT!

In 1 John 3:16 we ought also to lay down our lives for one another. This speaks of our soul life (mind, will, emotions) or not demanding our own way.

"All discipline for the moment seems not to be joyful, yet to those who have been trained by it, yields peaceful fruit of righteousness" (Heb 12:11).

"The fact that we are standing together in one spirit and one mind striving together for the faith of the gospel is a sign of destruction to the devil" (Phil 1:27,28).

We need, and must have, all three love relationships in our homes and marriages:

1. Phileo love is the friendship love. We enjoy being together.
2. Eros love is intimate/ sexual satisfaction
3. Agape love is a commitment not ruled by feelings and emotions.

Adam abandoned his relationship with God to assert his own independence. Men express their independence by turning to the work of their hands and sweat of their brow to find their identity, value and security. Goals and accomplishments are important to them. A quest for power equals security and significance.

The woman's desire is not to the works of her hands but, the woman in general will turn to the man to meet her need and for security..

Summary

Of major importance: The church and marriage was ordained and invented by God. That mighty, powerful church that Christ is coming after is made up of husbands, wives, and families.

As I have stated, Adam chose his own independence and gave up his relationship with God.. The only way that we can become that mighty, powerful Church is to regain that relationship. God came to earth and took upon Himself the form of man. Jesus lived among us and was crucified on the cross to pay the penalty (death) for Adam's (mankind's) sin. Now, we have the Holy Spirit to work in us and change our old adamic, carnal nature. *"All have sinned and come short of the glory (nature and character) of God"* (Romans 3:23).

As we yield our lives to the power of the Holy Spirit, we can be changed from glory to glory. We can develop that Christ-like nature and behavior in our lives. We can once again have that authority that Adam was given in the beginning.

God had a plan and He is still working that plan! He wants to use us, men and women, to do His will on this earth. He wants God to be seen in us. This will happen and it will start in our homes, as husbands and wives recognize each other as valuable in fulfilling that plan. We can re-present God to the world and it will start in our homes as we understand, appreciate and embrace the knowledge that men and women are different, special and have our own attributes of God!

We will appreciate and embrace our differences!

We can and will bring about that powerful church marching across the land doing the works of Christ.....this is His plan and His will.

WE CAN DO IT GOD'S WAY AND WIN!

THE END

Love Your Enemy!?

How do I do that?!

Foreword

God's amazing plan to reveal His love to a hurting world involves us, Christian believers and the Church of the Lord Jesus Christ. Not only are we to go and tell the world but we must also show them by our love. All men will know that we are His disciples if we love one another. We must be one that the world may believe that Jesus came from God.

To accomplish this has always seemed somewhat out of reach and idealistic: but God's Word will be fulfilled in these last days. A tremendous work of the Holy Spirit is going on and the stones of the temple are being prepared for assembly into a glorious church, and that joining together will be without the sound of hammer or chisel.

How do we forgive and love and grow in the Spirit? Latena Willis has been given some remarkable insights, revelations born of God within the crucible of human experience, and they are a wonderful blessing to believers.

For those seeking and perhaps struggling to obey God's second great command, "You shall love your neighbor as yourself," you have a useful tool.

Pastor W. Glenn McMurray
Bonney Lake, Washington

Love Your Enemy!?
How do I do that?!

Back when my husband & I were pastors of a church in the small town of Harrisburg, Oregon, he gave a Bible study on the gifts of the Spirit that made a lasting impression on me. He said, according to the Word, we should desire the gifts and he suggested that we look around and see which gifts were lacking in our church body. He asked that we begin to desire, pray and ask for those gifts.

The next morning, I turned to 1 Corinthians 12 and began to read and pray. Now, I happened to be reading out of the Living Bible and after Paul had gone through the gifts, at the end of chapter twelve, it read, *"First, however, let me tell you about something else that is better than any of them,"* and then chapter thirteen begins. My heart instantly began desiring love. Even though, this was not one of the nine spiritual gifts, there was no doubt that 'Love" was most lacking in the majority of the churches. Paul began to stress the fact that we could have all of these gifts, speaking in languages, prophecy, faith, even have all knowledge (this means we could even have the correct doctrines) and yet without love, we would only be making a noise!.

I began asking God to please give me love. I desired other gifts, but I wanted love more. I began to read everything I could find about love. Referring to Webster's dictionary plus other references, I learned the difference in:

1. **Philo,** love (to delight in, to be devoted to, have strong feelings or attraction for, friendship love)
2. **Eros** love (married love, physical, sexual)
3. **Agape** love (an action not based on feelings, but is based on commitment.)

There are many scriptures that refer to love:

"By this shall all men know that you are My disciples, if you have love one for another" (John *13:35).*

The mark of Christianity, in the very legalistic church I was raised in, was determined largely on outward appearance. However, in my research of the scriptures, the main criteria that seemed to be placed on us by Jesus is that of **love.**

"Love your neighbor as yourself" (James 2:8).

"Walk in love, just as Christ also loved you and gave Himself up for us" (Eph. 5:2).

"Love your enemies. If you only love those who love you, what profit is that? Even the sinners do this" (Luke 6:27-32).

"Through love, serve one another" (Gal. 5:13).

"God is love, and the one who abides in love abides in God, and God abides in him .... because as He is in the world, so also are we In this world. If someone says, I love God"* and hates his brother, he is a liar, for the one who does not love his brother... cannot love God. And this commandment we have from Him, that the one who loves God should love his brother also"* (1 Jn *4:16-21).*

"A new commandment I give to you, that you love one another, even as I have loved you, that you also love one another" (John *13:34).*

"Love is *a fruit of the Spirit* "(Galatians *5:22).*

The Lord allowed me to begin to "practice" love. Now, I thought since I had asked God for love, that I would have such great emotional ties or "feelings" for *everyone* and that I would not ever be offended and I would never, ever get my feelings hurt...etc. and since I was this way, guess what? Everyone would love me, too!! Right? *Wrong!*

Several experiences came my way and I found that I still battled with feelings. It was possible for others to hurt me and it was incredibly hard to keep my feelings under control. I felt that I was a complete failure. Try as I may, there were still people that I had trouble even liking, much less loving them! It seemed that Luke *6:27-38* was constantly "in my face". "Do you *think you deserve credit for merely loving those who love you? Even the godless do that. And if you only do good to those who do good to you is that so wonderful? Love your enemies.* " *I* find it easy to love those who pat me on the back and praise me, and the ones who bolster my ego. What about those who don't think I am so wonderful? I reasoned, "Let's face the facts, everyone has a different chemical makeup and there are just-those-who are not compatible. There will always be some personalities that will be irritable or just 'rub the wrong way' other personalities. That's just the way life is!"

Revelation!

NO ONE EVER EXPLAINED TO ME HOW IT WAS POSSIBLE TO LOVE MY ENEMIES!

One day I was crying out to God, feeling my inadequacy, not only as a pastor's wife, but as a Christian in general. I had my Bible open to Luke 6 and said, "Lord, this is impossible! How can I love my enemies? If I could love them, they would not be my enemy. I don't know how to do this!" The Lord said to me, "Read the rest of the verse." I knew what it said but I looked at it again, *"Do good unto them "* I said, "Lord, do you mean that I don't have to *like* them and I only have to do good to them?" I had felt like a failure because I could not *feel* a strong devotion, attraction or friendship for everyone, but maybe I could do this!

I had received a *revelation* from God! *God's love is not based on feelings but on an act of obedience to the will of God!* Jesus said, "My feelings didn't want to die on the cross. Three times I cried out, 'Father, if it could be your will, let this cup pass from me.'" Then He said, 'Never- the -less, not my will but Your will be done'". As an act of obedience to the will of the Father, Jesus by-passed His feelings and died on the cross for you and me .... while we were still sinners! We had never done anything to deserve salvation. We had not brought pleasure to God by loving him and being compatible to

Him or His purpose. We had not obeyed his commandments. He went to the cross for us while we were living in rebellion.

Love is a commandment, not a choice. *"This is my commandment that you love one another"* (John 15:10-12). God's commandments were not given to appease our five senses, our feelings, will, emotions. I found that there is never an opportune time to practice the gift of love. When we really need to **practice** love is when we really don't feel like doing it. I discovered that if I could by-pass my hurts and feelings and react to difficult situations in a manner that would bring pleasure to the heart of God, then I am loving. Agape love is based on a commitment and not a feeling. This is not easy to do because we are people who have been programmed all of our lives to react to our feelings, our senses. We must reprogram ourselves to live according to the Spirit man and to allow our reactions to complex situations to be in accordance to that which pleases God. As we begin to practice this kind of behavior, self control (another fruit of the Spirit) will be developed in our nature. This is all a part of God's plan to produce the fruit of the Spirit in our lives and the fruit of the Spirit is God's nature being developed in our character.

Every gift must be practiced and I found that I had many opportunities to practice love. I learned to pray for those with whom I had problems, to bless my enemy. When we ask God to bless, we are actually asking Him to interfere in their lives. We are not asking Him to give them everything they want but what they need. When WE bless others, it means we are to eulogize ... to say good things about them. I learned to be kind when my feelings wanted to do otherwise.

As I continued to practice the Word of God, I found that my feelings began to adjust. I was pleased to find that the Lord did not expect me to live void of feeling, however, I could not be controlled by feelings. My feelings must line up with the Word of God. I wondered if this was not being hypocritical ... to hide my feelings and "pretend" that "all was well". The Lord gave me the answer to this in one of Hannah Hurnard's books. She stated that it is never hypocrisy to behave in a manner that you truly want to feel! Isn't that great? If you truly would like to "feel" different, then your desires are good and God will help you through practicing His Word. Sometimes it takes time for our feelings to line up under the control of the Spirit Man, but this is the will and plan of God. This is Spiritual Maturity. Undeveloped or immature love causes one to walk in selfishness and to demand one's own way.

It is so necessary for us to experience the truths that the Lord reveals to us. Truth is never ours until we experience it and the result has been personalized, or made real within us and has become a part of us! We are His workmanship (Eph. 2:10) and He is working in our lives, not just to save us from hell and to take us to heaven, but rather to conform us to the image and likeness of Jesus Christ. As we begin to practice the truths that are revealed, our nature is changed!

We Make a Choice

A person is what he/she chooses to be. We can choose to walk in love. I am sorry to say that I have not always made the right choice. There have been times that I have chosen to gratify my feelings, to exercise "my rights", to satisfy my ego! After having a taste of walking in love, these episodes certainly left me with unhappiness, regret and a knowing that my choice was that which would only gratify the flesh and did not bring glory to my Lord.

"He who practices sin is of the devil/he who practices righteousness is of God" (1 Jn. 3:10). Verse 14 reads: *"We know that we have passed from death into life because we love the brethren."* This is a spiritual gauge. The world cannot see our love for Christ but they can see our love for each other. Jesus came to earth and lived among His people to show them the nature of God. Now, Jesus has returned to the heavens and has given us (his people) this task. We are to show the world God's nature! Is that a little scary to think that the world of humanity may be dependent on you and me to see God? Many times we must by-pass our own feelings, lay them aside to have harmony in our homes and our churches. This is mature love. I am not talking about becoming a "Yes" person, that we must not voice opinions or stand our ground as far as values, principles, etc. are concerned. I am speaking of attitudes. Love is not haughty or rude. Love does not demand its own way. There is never an excuse to be rude or unkind. It only takes a moment to be kind and it doesn't cost a dime. We

can disagree in a situation and stand our ground firmly and yet be kind and courteous.

This ministry of **love** is one we can use every day and it must begin at home! Husbands, love your wives! Wives, see that you show honor and respect to your husbands! Marriages that are built on human, natural love alone will not be happy and will more than likely end in the divorce courts. How many times have we heard the words, "I don't feel love anymore." Our feelings are changeable and fickle. When the **feelings** are not there and natural love is failing, it is at this time that we are to practice the Agape love (commitment love), until the feelings return. God's love is patient, kind, not jealous, is not arrogant, does not brag, does not act unbecomingly, does not seek its own, is not provoked, does not keep records of wrongs suffered and does not rejoice in unrighteousness. God's love bears all things, believes all things, hopes all things and endures all things. If both husband and wife are practicing God's love, you can be sure that the natural love will again be a part of this marriage!

The Church and Marriage are two institutions that are not only ordained by God but were invented by Him and they are important to Him. The Church is made up of families, husbands and wives, and this love must begin at home. The church will never be strong and in order if our marriages/homes are not strong and in order. *The ultimate purpose of God is to reveal His* **nature** *through His people and* to demonstrate His *power through His Church.* As we begin to practice His commandments, then we are changed. The problem is we want the power without the changed nature and it just does not work that way.

How can we Forgive?

Forgiveness is one of the hardest accomplishments of the Christian walk. All of my life I have heard sermons preached about forgiving those who have wronged us. My spirit would witness the truth of the matter. I would desire earnestly to forgive and not hold grudges. I listened as a preacher said, "Stop packing around things that you can't change! Just put those offenses down and forgive, get over it". This is good! How do you do this?

I found that when I pick up an offense or wrong that has been done to my husband or my children, this is the hardest to overcome. I can more easily forgive a hurt to me personally than a hurt to someone I love. I have really wrestled over some things. I would think that it was all right that I had "laid it down" and then when I would see that person, all of the injured, resentful feelings would surface. I realized that I still felt badly toward the individual. I wanted to feel different. I wanted to be able to forgive. Would someone please tell me how to do this! I didn't know how to forgive!

Many things cause separation in relationships ranging from personality conflicts, misunderstandings, hurt feelings, neglect, abuse, and deliberate wrongs committed against one another. Anything that comes our way that robs our sleep, joy, and peace should be dealt with immediately with forgiveness and love. This is our only choice. Anything short of this will produce stuff in our lives that will be burdensome to carry around such as anger, resentment, bitterness, rage, envy, jealousy, dislike, and in some cases, hatred. Each of these will rob us of God's presence, joy and peace.

The only access/influence that Satan has over us is through our five senses. He uses our feelings to his advantage. Many times it is our reactions to circumstances that cause us to be effective or ineffective, to hinder or to enhance our spirit-life. Satan does not have access to our spirit because our spirit has been united with God's Spirit but he can sure play havoc with our soul. We must take our feelings into control and not be controlled by our feelings. We can't wait for our feelings to change ... and then forgive. We must choose to forgive. Confess it, give it to God, ask Him to "love through us", then allow our actions to carry out our choice! Our feelings are a part of our soul, our five senses (feel, hear, see, sense, taste). God is in the business of restoring our soul. (Ps. 23:3) We are not to be soul-controlled but Spirit-controlled. As we yield our feelings to the work of the Holy Spirit, our feelings will come into line with His Spirit as we practice God's word until it becomes a part of our nature.

We do not have God's ability to forget sins. If I waited until I forgot about the offense, until I no longer hurt, until my feelings lined up, it would never happen. We are people so programmed by *feelings.* Our feelings are a part of our soulful nature. We cannot depend on or trust our feelings. We cannot lean on our own understanding but we must trust in the Lord! (Pr. 3:5) Following our feelings will lead us to destruction and a life of despair.

THIS IS THE WAY THE LORD HELPED ME TO FORGIVE. MAYBE IT CAN WORK FOR YOU.

Forgiveness is a choice! I choose to forgive! I want to *feel* different. I want to please God. I want freedom from this burden. I no longer want to carry around something that I can't change, so I speak it out in prayer to God. "I forgive this wrong and I forgive the person/persons involved in this injury to me or my loved one. I release this to you, Lord and ask that You forgive them also." The next time that I see this person, even though I remember the wrong and the same feelings come flooding over me, I have made a choice and I have chosen to forgive, so I exercise control over my behavior and behave as though the offense never happened! I take a step higher than my feelings and as an act of obedience to the will of God in my life, I take this opportunity to react to a difficult situation in a manner that pleases the Lord.

You must stop talking about the offense to others. It is as though it never happened. My husband and I have practiced this and in time, even though we do remember that an offense happened, it is hard for us to remember details because we ceased talking about it and did not keep records. You must be in control of your feelings and not controlled by them. A mature Christian is not controlled by feelings but by the word of God. If we do not allow ourselves to be controlled by feelings, we will find that our feelings will line up with the word of God. We want God to be glorified in our lives! *The ultimate purpose* of *God is to reveal His nature through His people and God is glorified when we are changed. We are changed as we practice His word!*

A person who is filled with pride will have a hard time practicing love and forgiveness. This person will demand and wait for apologies and will choose to exercise his/her rights and many times cannot even accept their own responsibility in the situation. In cases of this type, there is only one winner and that is Satan. A person with God's call in his/her heart cannot afford pride. A person with a dream or a vision in his/her heart cannot allow himself/herself to be offended. Hebrews 12:15 declares that bitterness can cause the grace of God to become short. Un-forgiveness and bitterness will disqualify us in the service of the Lord. Do *not become a casualty because of hurt feelings!*

Psalms 23: *"The Lord is my Shepherd, I shall not want. He makes me lie down in green pastures. Ile leads me beside quiet waters. He restores my soul. He guides me in paths of righteousness for His name sake."*

THE END

If I were the Devil....

We were in our yearly Full Gospel Fellowship meeting in Keizer, Oregon and I listened as Psalms 68:11 was read, "The women who proclaim the good tiding are a great army". The question was asked, "If you were the devil and knew this was in the Bible, what would you do?" It was suggested that you would possibly remind them that Paul wrote that women must be subdued and not teach.

I was intrigued with this thought, "If I were the devil...", and I thought that this "subdued plan" worked pretty good for a few hundred years but then in the early 1900's when the Holy Spirit was again poured out, women the same as men were consumed by the Holy Spirit of God and they could not/would not be quieted from the desire to spread the good news or to preach the gospel.

Now, if I were Satan and I knew the old trick wasn't cutting it anymore, what would I do then? I believe I would begin by organizing the ERA (Equal Rights). I would begin it innocent enough- equal pay for equal work. Then I would corrupt it with all kinds of "rights" jumping on the band wagon. I would organize the National Organization of Women (N.O.W.) and see that women without moral convictions, women who do not adhere to the teachings of the Bible were put in charge of this movement. With the FEMINIST movement in place, I would start an onslaught against the family with a plan to destroy homes.

I would like to share here with you some excerpts that I have gathered from articles and magazines:

A radical feminist who backs the ERA movement, Sheila Cronan, speaks for many of them, "Since marriage constitutes slavery for women, it is clear that the Women's movement must concentrate on attacking this institution. Freedom for women cannot be won without the abandonment of marriage." They want freedom from the burden of children. There can be no equality, they insist, as long as the woman is the homemaker. Moreover, the children, they say should be reared by another, namely the State. The Houston Conference for women sponsored by N.O.W. are calling for and pushing for federally funded day care centers around the clock, seven days a week. Society, they insist, as a whole should bear the burden of children.

Kate Millet writes that the family must go because it oppresses and enslaves women.

Divorce rate has risen over 700% in this century. Over 13 million children under 18 have one or both parents missing. Nearly 6 million pre-school children have working mothers and only a small fraction of these mothers work because of economic necessity.

Many colleges and universities convey a notion that the role of wife and mother is "passé", and to settle for such a role in life is to settle for second-class citizenship. The women's liberation movement has had an impact here. Though it focuses on some legitimate grievances, it appears eager to deny the responsibility of being a wife and mother. A home in which both parents are available to the child emotionally as well as physically has become the exception rather than the norm.

There has been a major increase in promiscuity and perversion... failure to control sexual urges, an increased incidence of homosexuality among young people and much greater freedom in expressing it.

Jean O'Leary wrote in the N.O.W. publication that Lesbianism should be taught in our schools and that school counselors should take courses in order to teach a positive view of lesbianism. A group in Boston called the Boston Boise Committee has been trying to convince the public that there is nothing "inherently wrong with sex between men and boys" and to lower the age of consent and change the child molestation laws to reduce legal barriers against such relationships.

This is a fact! There are forces in the world today out to cripple and to destroy our homes! These people are being driven by an evil force. They are militant in their demands! We must be aware of what is happening!

In our day we are seeing an all out assault on the family. It is coming from many different sources. We must be aware of these sources so that we can wisely build a spiritual "wall of protection" around our family and to build a strong base. We must be aware of the reason Satan is working overtime to destroy our homes. I might add here that it does not "take a village (government)" to raise our children. It takes a Mother and a Dad and a family to teach them needed values.

There are two institutions that are not only ordained by God but were invented by Him—Marriage and the church. If Satan can destroy our families, he can destroy the church. If families are out of order, then the church is out of order.

We can never be on a higher plane spiritually than we are in our homes. Who we are at home is who we are! We may go to church and put on a good "front" but it is who we are at home when there is no one around for us to impress that counts. (I have often thought the reason we were told to "go into our closets to pray" is because there it is just "God and me". I cannot impress God with my gifts and wordy prayers.)

Just as Satan began his attempt to massacre the plan of God in the garden, he approached Eve. He is still using the same plan today. He is approaching women and causing us to become restless and dissatisfied with God's plan for our lives. He uses the strength of our emotions to do his bidding, to usurp God's planned authority and to demand our own way. Perhaps if Eve would have discussed this temptation with Adam, he could have saved them and us a lot of heartache. She chose to make the decision on her own without the council or wisdom from her husband and this error has followed many women until today.

If I were the devil, for the next item on the agenda, I would see that the spirit of this FEMINIST movement enters the Church.! I would look around for special women of God, ones who have special gifts and ministries. I would whisper in her ear, tell her how great she is, I would point out her special gift and how she is being used of God. I would allow time for the spirit of pride to work in her. Then, I would suggest that she is so great and so used by God that she should just "take charge". She need not follow the chain of command set forth by God or accountability of the church. This is the same **tactic** that Satan used on Eve in the beginning—**the power strategy! You will be like God!**

Humanism is the 2nd oldest belief in the world and it began in the garden with Eve. Eve didn't ask council from Adam—or God. She just made the decision herself. If I were Satan, I would encourage this woman of God to rebel against authority as she begins to yield to this **take charge** spirit.

Women have been given a tremendous power of persuasion. We are masters at manipulation and we can use this power to build or to tear down...for good or evil. It is so important that we are aware of Satan's tricks. Let us be sure that our homes are into God's order!

There will be an army of women proclaiming the gospel but we will be doing it God's way! God has a plan and has set forth HIS chain of command (God, Jesus, man, woman) and He is not going to change it. Because of this, we as women need to realize that we are not less; only our purpose is different from that of a man's. We are special and are to have a special part in bringing about the return of our Lord. Our homes need-must have wives and mothers in them. **Not equal heads,** but a functioning part of the body— the heart, feelings, intuitions, understanding, compassion. We need to have an earthly focus on our family and an eternal focus on God, His will and His purpose for us. I truly believe that a nation's spiritual atmosphere is dependent on the spirituality of the women in that nation.

With this introduction in place, let's look at a way that we can retaliate against Satan's attempt to destroy our marriages and families as we focus on Titus chapter two. Paul was instructing Titus to encourage the older women to teach the younger women to love their husbands and to love their children. We need to return the basic of the scriptures and understand that we are called out from doing things the way the world does them. Women are the "hub" of the home!

Older women should teach younger women to:

1. Love Their Husbands

There are three (3) kinds of love. We must have all three of them in our home to have a successful marriage.

phileo love - friendship

eros - sexual

agape - commitment apart from feeling

Love is not only two people gazing into each other's eyes but two people looking in the same direction. Two people united with common goals, values and purpose and these goals, values, and purposes designed by God and set forth in His Word, the Bible.

Ways to Love our Husbands:

1. Be attractive: Pastor Robert Taylor says "take whatever you've got and do something with it!"
2. Be a friend: A good listener is invaluable at times.
3. Be fun to be with. Enjoy activities together.
4. Be a lover: Learn how to please your husband.
5. Be committed: even when you don't like him! This is where the agape love is so necessary. It takes us through the difficult times until the "feelings" are there again.
6. Give him quality time and attention.

7. Be a homemaker: Homes don't just happen. Make your home a pleasant place to be. Homes out of order are not pleasant, not only spiritually but physically. Make your beds, wash your dishes, do your laundry, keep it tidy!

Build "God confidence" in your husband. God does use him! He is a man of God. Encourage him to be the King and Priest of your home. Pray for him during the day as you are doing your work. Send him blessings and not curses as you speak of him. Speak of his strengths, not his weaknesses. Remember! He can become what you speak! Sometimes we have to "speak to things that are not as though they are". Rom. 4:17

Let him know that you appreciate him and that you submit to his leadership. Appreciate him as your covering and protector and let him know it! **You can build God confidence in your husband!** Encourage him! God can and does use him! He is a man of God! God didn't say to submit to him only if he is a strong spiritual leader. Allow him a chance to begin where he is!

Be a helpmeet (suitable) not helpmate (50-50)

Execute your husband's orders/desires even in his absence. This probably brings more honor to him than many other things which you could do and will cause respect for him to grow in the eyes of your children. There should be no double standards in your home. If you and your husband have differences of opinions, work it out between you. When you speak to your children or correct them, you should be united, not divided.

2. Love your Children:

Discipline them.

Teach them high moral values. (using God's Word as your reference source). Discuss with them issues confronting them today. If they don't hear your Godly opinions/values, they will hear it from other sources.

Uphold the teachings of the Bible on moral issues. God's word is the only absolute in the world today. Everything else is variable and subject to change. In the world today and especially with politicians and "liberals", the value system is based on "situation ethics". That means that you may change your "value system" according to popular demand. This means that your choice is justified because of the end accomplishment you are trying to reach. This means that you actually do not have conviction of your own. It is so important that we teach our children according to the scriptures.

Deal with the videos, movies, etc.

Pray for them.

Listen to them.

Never have double standards. It confuses children.

3. Keepers (guards) of the Home:

We have a managerial position. Take it seriously! It takes brains, time, and good sense to manage a family and do it well. God has qualified a woman for this special assignment—to keep the flow of traffic organized through the home with appointments, activities, shopping, groceries, nutritious meals, money management and council. **We have a humongous job to do and it is not to replace a man! A woman is the "hub" of the home!!**

4. Pure:

Faithfulness, goodness these are a part of the fruit of the Spirit. It is that quality in a woman who is ruled by and aims toward the quality of moral worth. Develop a perpetual desire and sincere study of the word. Choose to abstain from every appearance of evil and to do good to the utmost of your ability.

5. Kindness: (gentleness)

This, also, is a fruit of the Spirit. This kindness should pervade and penetrate our whole nature, mellowing in it all that is harsh and severe. Gentleness is a very rare grace, often wanting in many who have a considerable share of Christian excellence and abilities to minister in the gifts. A good education and polished manners when brought under the influence of the grace of God will bring out this trait of kindness with great effect. Gentleness is not rude. There is never an excuse to be rude. It doesn't cost a dime and it only takes a minute to be courteous. Rudeness is an expression of carnality and flesh and should be dealt with at once with repentance. It is rude to refuse to speak to or acknowledge another's presence.

6. Deny Ungodliness:

There is an army of women rising up today who are denying ungodliness. Only a few years ago in our textbooks, homo-sexuality was termed perversion, now we hear it called "alternate life style" or "the significant other". This is what the Bible teaches: "For this reason God gave them over to degrading passions; for women exchanged the natural function for that which is unnatural and in the same way also the men abandoned the natural function of the women and burned in their desire toward one another, men with men committing indecent acts and receiving in their own persons the due penalty of their error." (Rom. 1:26, 27) "Or do you not know that the unrighteous shall not inherit the kingdom of God? Do not be deceived; neither fornicators nor idolaters, nor adulterers, nor effeminate nor homosexuals, nor thieves, nor the covetous, nor drunkards,...shall inherit the kingdom of God" (I Cor.6:9). We need to hate sin as God hates sin! Abortion is now referred to as a woman's choice. Pornography has become common place. Permissive sex is accepted in our society today. We need to return to black and white...the grey areas have sin in them. We cannot follow the world's values!

The rods and cones in our eyes allow the eyes to adjust to darkness. Have you ever been reading a book outside and suddenly you realize it has actually gotten darker without your notice. Our eyes have the ability to adjust slowly to darkness. Satan has pulled the shades of our spiritual eyes down slowly on sin, not all at once. He allows us just enough time for our moral eyes to adjust to a little bit of grey in the white. In James 1:14,15, the word, "conception" is used in connection to sin. It takes 9 months for a baby to grow in its hidden place before it emerges for all of the world to see, but life began 9 months ago. "After desire (thought, lust) has conceived, it gives birth to sin." Between conception and birth there has been a time of quiet, slow, almost unnoticed development; then sin emerges and we wonder, "how did this happen?" Sin happened because the thought was entertained for a time before acted upon. Sin begins with a single thought.

7. Be subject to the Husband:

Submit is not a dirty word. It means to "pool" your resources to rally together for one purpose. It is **spiritual** to be a good wife and mother. This is the most important ministry or job in the eyes of God. Anything/any ministry that would separate you or hinder you in this position should be re-examined.

"Wives, submit to your husbands as unto the Lord." (Eph. 5:22) I refer to this as my **"as unto"** ministry".

"Wives, fit in with your husbands' plans - be beautiful inside in your hearts with the lasting charm of a gentle and quiet spirit which is so precious to God. That kind of deep beauty was seen in the saintly women of old who trusted God and fitted in with their husbands' plans. (I Pet 3:1-6)

"A single woman cares about the things of the Lord. A married woman's first ministry is to her husband." (1 Cor 7:34)

A mother who by her example in the home can instill a Christ-like nature and principles in her children and help her children to develop godly character and to experience a relationship with the Lord Jesus, this woman is spiritual!

When we are of one spirit and one mind striving together for the furtherance of the gospel it is **a sign of destruction to Satan!** Philippians 1:27,28.

If I were the devil, and could look and see husbands and wives united together in one spirit/mind striving together for the furtherance of the gospel, husbands loving their wives as Christ loved the church, wives respecting and submitting to the headship of the husband, children giving honor and respect in the home......**it would scare the devil out of me!**

We will become mighty because we order out ways before the Lord! 2 Chronicles 27:6.

Women! Let's do it God's way and win!!

The End

A Collection of

Inspirational Articles

When spending some time taking College Courses, I took a class, "Interpersonal Speech". In this class we talked about the art of listening. I was pretty impressed with this class and put together some thoughts along this line. Leon thought I might share it with you. I entitled my thoughts:

God's Transmitters-Intercessors Have Listening Hearts

"There is a conspiracy of her prophets in her midst, like a roaring lion tearing the prey. Her priests have done violence to my law and have profaned my holy things; they have made no distinction between the holy and the profane and they have not taught the difference between the unclean and the clean and they hide their eyes from my Sabbaths, and I am profaned among them. Her princes within her are like wolves tearing the prey, by shedding blood and destroying lives in order to get dishonest gain. And her prophets have smeared whitewash for them seeing false visions and divining lies for them saying, 'thus says the Lord God' when the lord has not spoken. The people of the land have practiced oppression and committed robbery and they have wronged the poor and needy and have oppressed the sojourner without justice, and I searched for a man among them who should build up the wall and stand in the gap before me for the land that I should not destroy it; but I found no one." Ezek 22:24-30

"But your iniquities have made a separation between you and your God, and your sins have hidden His face from you, so that He does not hear.....Your lips have spoken falsehood, your tongue mutters wickedness. No one sues righteously and no one pleads honestly. They trust in confusion and speak lies, they conceive mischief and bring forth iniquity....Their works are works of iniquity, and an act of violence is in their hands. Their feet run to evil and they hasten to shed innocent blood; their thoughts are thoughts of iniquity;....they do not know the way of peace and there is no justice in their tracks; they have made their paths crooked; whoever treads on them does not know peace. Therefore justice is far from us for our transgressions are multiplied before Thee, and our sins testify against us...speaking oppression and revolt...justice is turned back and righteousness stands far away....truth is lacking and he who turns aside from evil makes himself a prey. Now the Lord saw and it was displeasing in His sight that there was no justice and He **saw that there was no man and was astonished that there was no one to intercede"** (Isa. 59:9-16).

Does it seem that you could be reading the above from the headlines of one of our daily newspapers? The same violence, crime, oppression and corruption are common in this Christian country in our day! And God saw it, and He wondered that there was "no intercessor". Notice that God did not wonder that there was no one He could use as a great reformer or revivalist, or deliverer....but there was no intercessor!

Ezekiel said that He looked for a man to stand in the gap, to join up a broken place and Isaiah was told that God was looking for an intercessor (maphgia) someone to bring two separate things together so that they should meet again and be in contact.

Intercessor: I use to think in order to be an intercessor, meant that I would be spending hours daily on my knees, crying out to God for the needs of the people.

Rather, let us look at an "intercessor" as someone to be a means of contact or conductor of power to bridge the gap which has come in the relationship between God and His people.

An intercessor is one who is in vital contact with God and in touch with his fellow men so that he is like a live wire closing the gap between the saving power of God and the ones who have been cut off from that power....a connecting link between the source of power (life of Jesus) and the objects needing that power. **We are to be a transmitter of His life and power and love to others.**

When we are united with our Lord Jesus and have a love and compassion for the people, we are literally the means which God

can and does use to reach the minds and wills of those who are cut off.

1. We have heard the expression of being so spiritually minded that we are of no earthly good. Well, I don't think we can be too spiritual....it is possible that our skills of communication and reaching people need some help.
2. There are others who have a good rapport with people, good communication skills, sincere interest and compassion, but not a vital relationship with God
3. An intercessor/transmitter lives in vital contact with God (the power source) through faith and has the ability to communicate that power through love to people.

Example: Lot was living, apparently, as a godly man by profession. He was a good man. He was a believer but he was out of contact with God, and out of contact with his fellow man...He could not bridge the gap and become a conductor by means of which the saving power of God could reach the people of the cities.

We are called to be transmitters of the power of Christ (the anointed) perhaps not as an evangelist, a minister or a reformer, but to those whom we come into contact daily—a one to one ministry! We can have that anointing because we have contact and communication with the Anointed One.

We are going to zone in on one way to improve our ministry as transmitters of the power of God...by being better listeners to those with whom we come into contact.

Listening is a skill much like speaking, everyone does it, but few do it well!

How are we doing as a communicator? Are we good listeners?

Transmitters are communicators! Communication is so important as we attempt to influence others, or win others into the Kingdom of God. The people who know, tell us that 61% of our time is spent in communication and 42% to 63% of time is spent listening and yet people today spend lots of dollars paying someone to LISTEN to them. We all desire to make our time of communication as effective as possible. Right? It is up to us to create a favorable "climate" as we do our best to communicate with those whom we come into contact daily.

We can create a "positive climate" of communication when we cause the other person to feel our concern about their welfare. A positive response will cause the other person to feel valued, acknowledged and that their importance is confirmed. A positive response will give a feeling of trust. A "negative climate" is created when we give the feeling of unimportance, neglect or abuse; when we deny the importance or even the existence of another's presence.

We are not likely to say to others "you are inferior" or "you are not important" but messages are communicated by interrupting or ignoring the other person's attempt at communication. We send messages to another by:

1. Verbally-non/verbally (by butting into conversation or turning your back to the speaker.) I was speaking at a Faith Family camp meeting and was teaching on "Love". There was a man in the audience who, evidently, didn't like me or what I was saying, he stood up, turned his chair around and sat down with his back to me. Now that truly made a statement!

2. Ignoring or disregarding the person's attempt to communicate.
    (Children receive this response a lot.)

3. Interrupting - one person begins to speak before the other one is through making a point.

4. Irrelevant - this involves comments totally unrelated to what the other person was saying.

5. Tangential (touching a curved surface but not connecting) - this is using the conversation to steer in another direction. A tangential drift makes a token connection of what the other

person was saying but slowly moves the conversation into his/her direction.

To become a better communicator, we need to be a better listener! Psychology and psychiatry are in demand today because of the need for someone to listen! From kindergarten to college, students receive instruction in reading, writing and even speaking but there is an almost total lack of instruction in listening! **Listening is a skill much like speaking, everyone does it, but few do it well!**

Myths about Listening:

1. <u>Hearing and Listening are the same thing.</u> Hearing is a process where sound waves strike the ear drum and cause vibrations that are transmitted to the brain and gives them meaning. Baring illness/injury, you hear whether you want to or not. Listening is a choice. We can block irritating sounds or subjects that are not interesting or unimportant to us - for example, TV commercials, stories, complaints, background noises.

2. <u>Listening is a Natural Process.</u> As stated earlier, listening is a choice. Listening is a skill and few people do it well.

3. <u>All Listeners receive the same message.</u> Each listener perceives an event in a different manner depending upon:
Physiological factors (feelings at the moment)
Social roles
Cultural backgrounds
Personal interest

Listening is a choice and a person's needs, wants, desires and interest determines what he/she listens to. For example, when I was attending college, I would go into the cafeteria between classes to study. The noise was terrible, yet I was able to go, sit at an end of a table with all kinds of conversations going on all around me, turn it off and concentrate on my studies. One day, there was a young man talking to another about Jesus and making a plea for salvation. I absolutely was unable to "turn off" this conversation because of my interest and knowledge in the subject discussed. **Our Understanding Depends on:** our knowledge and interest about the subject; our social context and our common assumptions.

Poor Listening Habits!

Most people possess one or more bad listening habits. Which one describes you?

1. PSEUDO LISTENING -imitation of the real thing, pretend to be interested but something entirely different going on in your thoughts. You are either pre-occupied or bored. This is counterfeit communication! Everyone day-dreams sometimes while listening to others, but if you dream a lot with certain people it may indicate a lack of commitment to them or getting to know them.

2. STAGE HOGGING - only interested in expressing their own ideas and don't care about what anyone else has to say. Only let others speak from time to time while they catch their breath. Stage Hogs do not converse, they only "make a speech". Stage Hogs compare. "I have had it harder than you or I could do it better than you". Stage Hogs identify. "I know just how you feel" or "I had the same thing happen to me..." They take what a person says and refer it back to THEIR past and THEIR experience rather than the person telling the story and switch the subject from that person to themselves.

3. SELECTIVE LISTENING - they respond only to the parts of the speakers remarks that interest them, rejecting everything else until the subject turns to their favorite subject.

4. FILLING IN THE GAPS - people remember half or less of what they hear. Some people manufacture information so they can retell what they listened to and can give the impression "they got it all". This is as dangerous as selective listening. It is a distorted version of the message.

5. INSULATED LISTENING - (my grandchildren do this) This is opposite of selective listening. When a topic arises they don't want to deal with, they fail to hear or acknowledge. Just nod or answer you and then forget it.

6. DEFENSIVE LISTENING - take innocent comments as personal attacks. Examples: teenagers with questions about their friends; insecure breadwinners about money; a wife who is insecure as a manager; someone with a weight problem; parents about authority with children; anytime you are looking to prove a point. It is assumed that defensive listeners are suffering from shaky images.

7. AMBUSH LISTENING - listen carefully because they are collecting information that they will use to attack what you say. Example: Lawyers for cross-examining; a person with an offense.

8. INSENSITIVE LISTENING - Not able to look beyond the words and behavior to understand the hidden meanings. They take the speakers remarks at face value. Example: husband/wife argument - how many times have we rapidly fired accusations at each other, both talking at the same time and constantly interrupting each other with every word driving a wedge deeper into the relationship. The wife says, "get out of here and leave me alone", but really she is crying in her heart, "put your arms around me and help me to get over this."

9. PLACATING - you want people to like you so you always try to please and agree with everything.

HOW TO LISTEN MORE EFFECTIVELY AND BECOME A BETTER RECEIVER

I have been writing a few things concerning the art of listening. We have discussed the "Myths about listening", "Poor listening habits"(most people possess one or more bad listening habits). At this time we will zone in on "how to listen more effectively and become a better receiver".

1. STOP TALKING! Zero in on what is being said. We have been given two ears and one mouth! REALLY LISTEN! Do not silent debate, rehearse

and retort in your mind. Try to understand the person's viewpoint without necessarily agreeing with it. It is important that we know (understand) something about the other person's viewpoint and values.

2. PUT THE SPEAKER AT EASE-create a supportive communication climate by using non-verbal clues, good eye contact, lean forward, use a warm tone of voice.

3. REACT APPROPRIATELY-offer positive or negative feedback (nodding, shaking your head, verbal expressions) as you respond. Listen for the speaker's feelings, values, attitudes, judgment and needs.

4. CONCENTRATE ON WHAT THE SPEAKER IS SAYING, focus on the words, ideas, and feelings of the speaker. Pay attention to the tone of voice, facial expressions, etc. Put speaker's ideas in your own words and relate them to your own experience (without switching the attention from them to yourself.) Reflect back to the sender what you hear being said.

5. GET RID OF DISTRACTIONS AND AVOID FIDGETING

6. AVOID INTERRUPTING UNTIL THE OTHER PERSON EXPRESSES A COMPLETE THOUGHT. How frustrating to have someone interrupt you in the middle of your sentence, thinking that he/she knows what you're about to say and then jumping to a conclusion! We have all done that at times. We have jumped to "illusions" about what the person was actually saying. We've heard the words that were spoken, but we didn't really listen to what was being said and what misunderstandings have resulted!

> Respectful listening keeps anger under control and promotes righteousness. Let's listen carefully and avoid jumping to "illusions".

I can't imagine that Jesus ever engaged in discourteous conversation. People listened to Him and He listened to them. James wrote in his letter to the early church, "Be swift to hear, slow to speak, slow to wrath". James 1:19, I am sure he saw this modeled in Jesus many times over!

7. AVOID MAKING ASSUMPTIONS, ASK QUESTIONS

8. DON'T ARGUE MENTALLY-give a fair hearing, if you argue mentally you cannot concentrate on what the speaker is saying.

9. LISTEN FOR MAIN POINTS AND SUPPORTING EVIDENCE

10. SHARE RESPONSIBILITY FOR THE COMMUNICATION-communication is a transaction. Ask questions, receive thoughts and feelings accurately. Remember how often people have misunderstood you while you felt certain that they knew what you meant? A good active listener will paraphrase a statement that reflects both your feelings and thoughts.

EVERYONE NEEDS AT LEAST ONE FRIEND WHO IS A GOOD LISTENER!

I was reading in 1 Chronicles 27, it was listing the various overseers of David's kingdom and I stopped at the 33rd verse. "and Hushai the Archite was David's friend." What a legacy! Hushai was not even an Israelite. I could only imagine the hours that surely this man spent listening to David. David must have felt secure in this man's confidence. He could reveal his heart, his dreams, his fears, his failures, his hopes! Even Kings need a true friend. Everyone needs a true friend...**even pastors and pastors' wives!**

A person will communicate determined by the degree that they see themselves valued!

IT IS EASY TO LISTEN TO WORDS THAT ARE SAID AND NOT HEAR THE FACTS AT ALL BUT LISTENING FOR TRUTH, AND NOT JUST TO WORDS WILL **SAVE** YOU FROM MANY A FALL! -Hess

You can win more friends with your ears than with your mouth.

To become God's transmitter/intercessor to the world around us, we must learn how to effectively touch those around us with God's love. "By this shall all men know that you are My disciples, if you have love one for another". St John 13:35

There are two things which the Lord emphasized all through His teaching:

1. The supreme importance of faith as the only way to make contact with God.

2. Love as the one vital principle by which we maintain contact with our fellow man. All of the practical teachings our Lord gave in connection with the lives that we are to live here on earth are summed up in the commandment to love.

A lot of money is paid everyday to Psychologist - Psychiatrist from people who need someone to listen to them, not only to listen but to keep confidence. We need to practice not only the art of listening but the art of friendship!

THE END

The New Birth

1 Peter 1:23 "For you have been born again not of seed which is perishable but imperishable, that is, through the living and abiding word of God"

A. The new birth involves our spirits and can happen through believing and faith without feeling and emotion. Our spirits are joined with God's Spirit and we will live forever. Most people look for and expect feelings. Many times this does come with feelings of joy, peace and anticipating, however, the new birth will happen because of faith, not feeling.

B. We have been born again! Our spirit has united with His Spirit by faith. Now our soul comes into attention. This is not an instant happening....our mind, will and emotions have to be renewed. It would be great if a magical, mystical happening took place at the same time and suddenly we were different, like perfect. It does not happen!.

C. We wake up the next morning in the real world and realize that a war has been declared! We do not wake up in a rose garden, but a battle field! We must yield our mind, will and emotions to the word of God. We must pray and trust the Holy Spirit to help us make different choices. Our minds become the battlefield. God's Spirit on the inside of us is a battering ram, knocking down strongholds in our nature! GOD HAS A PLAN FOR US!

"For it is God who is at work in you causing you to desire to do His will"
(Philippians 2:13).

1. We cannot depend on our feelings...they are fickle.

2. We cannot depend on our thinking and reasoning
Example: The story in Deuteronomy 1:20: "You have come to the hill country of the Amorites which the Lord our God is about to give us. The Lord your God has placed the land before you; go up and take possession as the Lord, the God of your fathers, has spoken to you. Do not fear or be dismayed. Moses said, 'all of you approached me and said let us send some men to go before us and look it over' and this pleased Moses and he took 12 men, 1 from each tribe.....they came back with fruit from the land and gave a report that it is good land that the Lord has given to them. They refused to go up and take the land because the people were bigger and their cities fortified Moses encouraged them to go up, reminding them of how the Lord has fought for them and brought them here...but for all of this, you did not trust the Lord your God."

3. They failed because of their own thinking and reasoning. One of the first things we have to deal with is our mind, our thinking. **We must trust in the lord with all of our hearts and lean not to our own understanding (5 senses) and he will make our paths straight**. Proverbs 3:5

Many of our problems, we have created for ourselves—spiritual, mental, physical and financial.

What we perpetually believe, picture in our mind, this gets into our spirit and that is who we are. Sometimes we may have to overcome something that was told us as children. Proverbs 23:7 As a man thinks, so is he.

These are not the fleeting thoughts or moods that alter from day to day but our inner thoughts that we may not disclose to others but believe ourselves. These shape us.

4. The Holy Spirit is an experience that involves our emotions. Paul says that we will receive power after the Holy Spirit is received!

The first thing we need power over is our own soul, our mind, will, emotions. We need help to change our thinking!

Satan uses our mind, if you think his thoughts or allow him to think through you, you will began to manifest his behavior.. Be wise of his tricks.

This brings about the importance of a Church life! The Church was God's idea! There is a purpose for the Church. We receive fellowship, strength, spiritual nourishment. Be in fellowship, be teachable, learn what the word of God says and begin to practice the word whether you feel like it or not.

Refuse to be controlled by feelings. Remember Jesus in the garden? His feelings did not want to go to the cross. He asked three times if this could be taken away, but then he said "Not my will but your will be done" and as an act of obedience to the Father, he suffered the cross for you and me.

It is up to us to put new thoughts and directions into control. We have the power of the Holy Spirit to help us. Yield to it.

Discover ways to please God in your daily life.

Obey his commandments. (These were not given to appease our five senses but to change us!)

We love our enemies...not by feeling, but by doing good to them. Luke 6:27.

We choose to forgive and even though we remember the wrong when we see that person, we have made a choice and behave as though the wrong never happened. As you practice this, your feelings will change!

We practice the word of God until it becomes a part of our nature. This is how we are changed.

It is awkward and uncomfortable for us to "put aside our old self". Colossians 3:8-16.

YOU, put aside your old self: anger, wrath, malice, slander, abusive speech, lying. We are to lay aside our old self with its evil practices and put on our new self who is being renewed to a new knowledge according to the image of God. Verse 12, We have been chosen of God! We are to put on: a heart of compassion, kindness, humility, gentleness, patience and bearing with one another, forgiving one another and above all else, we are to put on love. Verse 16, Let the word of Christ dwell in your hearts!

Jesus came to show us God. He left us the Holy Spirit and now it is our turn to show the world Christ! The ultimate purpose of God is not to save us to keep us from going to hell but to reveal His nature to a world! The world is waiting for the CHURCH to manifest this glorious nature.

Romans 8:4-14

Verse 6. The mind set on the flesh (old nature) is death. The mind set on the Spirit is life and peace.

Verse 8. Flesh (carnality) cannot please God.

Verse 10. Our spirit is alive because of righteousness (we stand righteous before God)

Verses 12, 13 By the Spirit (our battering ram) we are putting to death the old nature.

1st Corinthians 2: 11-16 The natural man does not accept the things of the Spirit...they are foolish to him.

Romans 12:2 Do not be conformed to the world but be transformed (changed) by the renewing of your mind.

2nd Corinthians 10:3-5 We are taking every thought captive to the obedience of Christ. We are not controlled by our thoughts but we are **in control** of our thoughts!

Proverbs 25:28 A person with no rule over his/her own spirit (mind-5 senses) is like a city without walls.

I thought this information was interesting and worthy of consideration:

The way an Elephant is trained: Elephant verses the stake:

1. The elephant is tied to a stake in a way that whenever he would resist it, caused pain.

2. He began to accept it and as time went by smaller/smaller stakes are used and then portable ones.

3. Finally the stake becomes his master. In his mind he remembers the pain and never   challenges it again. It became his stronghold

4. This powerful huge elephant is held in bondage to a small stake in the ground.

Satan will put wrong thoughts into your mind in an attempt to trick you into his kingdom.

The one who has an undisciplined thought life will have an undisciplined behavior!

Start with one thing at a time and work on it!

What is the stake in your life?

What is holding you bound?

What is keeping you from a mountain goat experience....fear, peer pressure, perverted thoughts, sickness, inferiority, sex, alcohol, un-forgiveness, secret sins.....?

Christians were set free 1900 years ago! We have the power and authority over all the power of the enemy! Don't let him continue to think through you!

If we think Satan's thoughts, the result is his behavior.

If we think God's thoughts, the result is His behavior.

Whatever we focus on that is who we become.

Too much of the time, Christians have become a reproach because we have not understood that our changed behavior is not an instant thing that happens when we are saved. It is a process! We need to let revelation happen!

Romans 8:29: It is His will that we become conformed to His nature.

Good deeds will glorify you personally...a changed nature will glorify God!

Our influence to a world that needs Christ is not the law of do's and don'ts but a changed nature. I grew up in religion - a lot of do's and don'ts, especially geared toward women: no make-up, no jewelry, no pants, can't cut hair...no movies. I was told that as you are walking down the street, people should be able to look at you and know that you are a Christian. I was still a little girl when I asked the question, "How can you tell if a man is a Christian?" They looked like any other man walking down the street. Well, I am so thankful that God has delivered us from religious bondage!

Take it one step at a time and personally find ways for you to please God! Habits are formed by practice...and our natures will be changed as we practice doing God's word!

"AS UNTO" MINISTRY

"Wives, submit yourselves unto your own husbands **as unto the Lord**"
Eph.5:22

In today's modern society with women "libbers" running rampant and the National Organization of Women attacking the institution of marriage (Sheila Cronan speaks for many of them "since marriage constitutes slavery for women, it is clear that the Women's movement must concentrate on attacking this institution. Freedom for women cannot be won without the abolition of marriage".), it is easy to lose sight of the plan of God in marriage and family living. If families are out of control and marriages are not following the divine order of God, how can the Church of today possibly come into God's divine maturity since the Church is made up of husbands, wives and children.

This feminist spirit has entered the Church to a great extent. In the Church world today, we as women have looked around to the right and to the left in search of a ministry and many have felt "unfulfilled" unless we have a "recognized" ministry and have many times neglected our most important God given ministry....**our own husband.**

This ministry is more than putting nutritious meals on the table, doing the laundry, dishes, keeping our home tidy. Even though, all of these physical "duties" are a part of our ministry. Let us take a look at other ways that we can minister to our husband. First, we will seek for ways to please him. We will plan time to be alone with him and to give him quality time and attention.

Several years ago as my daughter was preparing to be married, someone had given her a book to read entitled "Total Woman". I had heard of the book and thought I would read it. As I picked the book up, I felt the Lord said to me, "Put it down, I don't want you to read it." I did not understand and questioned the Lord about this and I feel this is the answer He gave to me. "Too many times women will pick up books that are designed to teach women how to please their husbands and when they implement different ideas and plans that are suggested in the book and their husbands do not respond in the way the husband in the book responded, it causes frustration and more problems." Every man is unique and totally different. The Lord told me that He knew my husband and that HE would help me to know how to please him. So wives, seek for ways to please your husband and if you need help, ask the Lord. HE is interested in your marriage and your relationship. He is the one who invented and ordained marriage and HE desires that our lives be fulfilled and happy. Didn't He say that we could cast all of our cares upon HIM because HE cares for us? Anything in our lives that concerns us, concerns HIM!

Another way that we can minister to our husbands AS UNTO THE LORD is through our praises and blessings. All during the day we can send blessings to our husbands. Is it possible that our husbands can become what we say? So shall we send blessing or cursing? When we speak of his weaknesses or say negative, unkind things about him, we are speaking curses upon him. To begin with, we may even have to "speak of things that are not as though they are", but if we are obedient to the word of God and continue ministering to our husbands in blessings and praise, we will see a change! It is OK to praise your husband! Don't dwell on all of the faults that he may have but look at his good points and begin to compliment him and praise him. Remember, the Word doesn't say to submit to your husband if he is perfect, if he is a strong spiritual leader and has great wisdom and knowledge, but in spite of the imperfections that he may have, praise him and bless him and thank the Lord for him and for the work that HE is doing in your husband. Let your husband know that you are honored to trust in his leadership. Respect is one of His greatest needs. Give him that respect. Women have been given a tremendous power of persuasion and we can use it to build up or to tear down. You can build God confidence in your husband! If he is a born again believer, allow him to begin his spiritual leadership of the home right where he is and give him the assurance that you are standing with him.

Remember, your husband is your number one ministry! This is a special ministry because no one else can minister to your husband in the same effective way that you can. I don't know about you, but I most assuredly would not want anyone else to minister to my husband in my place, therefore, it is very important that I serve in this ministry to the very best of my ability.

Recently, while attending a wedding and listening as the wedding vows were being exchanged, I was reminded of Paul's writings in 1st Corinthians 7, "the woman who is unmarried is concerned about the things of the Lord, how she may please the Lord; but one who is married is concerned about the things of the world, how she may please her husband." Paul didn't say this was wrong, or that a married woman is a second class Christian , that is just how things are. When we choose to become married, our marriage should always be our most important ministry. In fact, I personally believe that we cannot neglect our marriage and our home and please God.

As we seek to fulfill this ministry of love toward our mates and become comfortable and contented in this ministry, it is possible that other doors of ministry will be opened to us and as we begin to reach out in other ways to other people, let us never forget our most important and our number one ministry...OUR OWN HUSBAND! **Any ministry that would interfere with the ministry to your own husband should certainly be questioned**. Remember! No one can minister to your husband as you can. Love him, bless him, praise him, seek for quality time to spend with him, let all of the menial task that you do become a ministry of love and service....AS UNTO THE LORD!

Dancing with God

Guidance -giving direction/leadership
Guide-lead or train
Dance-rhythmic movement

Have you ever thought about or meditated on the word "guidance"?

I looked it up in the dictionary and it has reference to leadership - someone who leads. I kept seeing the word "dance" at the end of the word. I remember reading that doing the will of God is a lot like dancing!

Only one can lead. When two people try to lead, nothing feels right. The movement doesn't flow with the music and everything is uncomfortable and jerky. When one person realizes this and lets the other lead, both bodies will begin to flow with the music.

I have always enjoyed watching as couples dance together. Especially couples who have danced together for years, they move as one person! Amazing!

Leon and I have never danced, so I asked my brother, Perry and Leon's brother, Clyde about how the one who leads gives cues to his partner. One can give gentle cues, perhaps with a nudge to the back or by pressing a direction with a hand. Sometimes even a more intimate way, pulling your partner closer and whispering in her ear. The one following needs to know and understand cues of steps and direction....and you can only follow one. I think it would be difficult to follow one if your attention is on someone else! Right?

We must be aware of who has our attention. Who has your attention has you! Your faith can be controlled by who or what has your attention.

To dance with God, God must have our attention! We need to learn about Him and His ways. We must develop a relationship with Him by reading His word, we will begin to understand His ways, also as we meet with Him in conversation (prayer) and allow Him to guide us through our lives. We will learn to trust His leading.

One way that He wants to lead us, to give us nudges and cues in life is through our minds, thoughts. Not every thought comes from God, but you will learn His voice and as you learn the scriptures, you will compare what you have heard in your thoughts with what is taught through the word of God. 1st Corinthians tells us that the natural man cannot understand things of the Spirit, but we who have learned about Him understand spiritual things because we have the mind of Christ.

We take control of our thoughts. 2nd Corinthians 10:5 "and we are taking every thought captive to the obedience of Christ."

Isaiah 30:21...and your ears will hear a word behind you, "this is the way, walk in it"

I have always loved psalm 1:1 "Blessed (empowered to succeed) is the man who does not walk in the counsel (guide, advice, suggestion) of the ungodly, nor stand in the path (course in life) of sinners (those outside of God), nor sit in the seat of the scoffers (distraction), but his delight (pleasure, desire, pursuit) is in the law (instruction, direction) of the lord and in his law he meditates day and night ....verse 3.... in whatever he does, he prospers.

Romans 12:1,2 ....present your bodies a living and holy sacrifice (going places and doing things you don't want to do...my personal interpretation :^)) acceptable to god, which is your spiritual service of worship. And do not be conformed (adapt) to this world but be transformed (be changed, reprogrammed .... and it is a process) by the renewing of your mind that you may prove what the will of God is, that which is good , and acceptable and perfect (complete).

Romans 6:12 therefore do not let sin reign in your mortal body that you should obey its lusts, (verse 13) and do not go on presenting the members of your body to sin as instruments (weapons) of unrighteousness; but present yourselves to God as those alive from the dead and your members as instruments (weapons) of righteousness to God. Verse 16 tells us that whoever we "present" our bodies to , we become slaves of the one we obey or follow.

John 14:4 Jesus tells us that his sheep know his voice and another they will not follow.

As you take your eyes back to the word Guidance, you see the "G"...think of God, followed by "U" and "I". I continually strive to trust that we will have GUIDANCE in our lives. Now, more than ever before I am willing to let God lead. I am willing to acknowledge the importance of the sovereignty of God. He knows a lot more than I do and I can trust Him. Sometimes I have felt that God has had to "step on my toes" to get my attention! :^)

My prayer today is that God's blessings and mercies be upon us this day and every day. May we abide in God as God abides in us. Let us dance together with God, trusting God to lead and to GUIDE us through each season of our lives.

I trust you pray this prayer with me and I hope you DANCE WITH GOD.

Psalm 23:3 "He restores my soul (my mind, will, emotions). He GUIDES me in the path of righteousness for His name sake".

John 16:12 "When He, the Spirit of truth has come, He will GUIDE you into all truth..."

Let us make the decision to dance with Jesus for the rest of our lives and let him lead!

Life will be sweet!

The Silk Worm

Recently, while we were in Los Angeles, we were staying in the home of Cathy Young, a young lady from China. China is famous for its silk industry. I asked Cathy questions about this because I have always been intrigued and amazed that beautiful silk is spun by caterpillars! I then came home and looked up SILK on the internet. I will share with you some thoughts and information concerning the miracle work of the silkworm!

SILK, the fabric that makes its own statement! Say "silk" to someone and what do they visualize? No other fabric generates quite the same reaction. For centuries silk has had a reputation as a luxurious fabric, one associated with wealth and success. Silk is one of the oldest textile fibers know to man. It has been used by the Chinese since the 27th century. During the Roman Empire, silk was sold for its weight in gold.

Today silk is yet another word for elegance and silk garments are prized for their versatility, wear ability and comfort. Silk is the strongest natural fiber,... a steel filament of the same diameter as silk, will break before a filament of silk. Silk absorbs moisture, which makes it cool in the summer and warm in the winter. Because of its high absorbency, it is easily dyed in many deep colors. Silk retains its shape, drapes well, caresses the figure and shimmers with a luster all of its own.

Silkworms possess a pair of specially modified salivary glands called sericteries which are used for the production of silk cocoons. These glands secrete a clear, viscous, proteinous fluid that is forced through openings called spinnerets on the mouthpart of the worm. As the fluid comes into contact with the air it hardens. The diameter of the spinneret determines the thickness of the silk thread. The larvae fed on mulberry leaves produces the best silk. The larvae will eat 50,000 times its initial weight in plant material. After it has reached its maximum growth at 7.5 cm at around 4-6 weeks it stops eating, attaches itself to a twig, tree or shrub and begins to spin its cocoon.

I can imagine these little worms as miniature bulldozers eating everything in sight and after they have finished eating, they began swaying drawing figure 8 (eight) in the air, they are ready to spin. Suddenly from the spinneret on the silkworm's under lip, a thin delicate thread of pure silk appears and it sways rhythmically, tracing the movement of the silkworm's body. Can you imagine being able to spin pure silk right out of your body? During this time of spinning, something else is taking place....metamorphose.

1. A caterpillar can spin silk out of its own substance and transform itself into something beautiful - a butterfly.

2. We, as children of God, can change coarse living into the fine fabric of life. We can transform bitterness into something sweet, hatred into love, un-forgiveness into forgiveness.

3. We can grow into a gentler more beautiful being - like the caterpillar.

4. Caterpillars leave their silk behind them.
   They take something inside them and turn it into silk
   They do not stay in their cocoons
   They come out and leave their silk behind for
   Every one else to enjoy
   They never want it back

Let us spin a little silk out of the substance of our lives. Leave it behind us wherever we go. Don't look back into the cocoon you made. Go forward into life and watch the person you become reflect the beauty you leave behind.

Just as it is important for the caterpillar to eat a special diet, it is also important that we take into our spirit and senses proper nourishment! I am thinking of the scripture that says that man should not live by bread alone but by every word that proceeds from the mouth of God. Eating from the word of God will provide us spiritual nutrition. We are also taking in spiritual nutrition during times of praise and worship. We are taking in spiritual nutrition as we fellowship with one another. We are being nourished today as we meet together. This nutrition, the Word, Praise, Worship, and Fellowship will surely cause the spirit-person within us to produce quality attributes and help us to metamorphose (be transformed). This happens to us as we mature in our Christian life and it is then that Christ is seen in us. We re-present Christ. We are not to wait to be changed "on the way up" but we will be changed here and now as we take in good nutrition and put to practice God's word. His commandments were not given to us to appease our five senses but to change us. Example: To love one another is not a choice it is a commandment. We love not according to feelings but as an act of obedience. God is glorified as we are changed into His image.

I would like to consider Philippians 4:4-8:

"Rejoice in the Lord always; again I will say, rejoice! Let your forbearing (gentle) spirit be known to all men. The Lord is near. Be anxious for nothing, but in everything by prayer and supplication with thanksgiving let your request be made known to God and **the peace of God**, which surpasses all comprehension (capacity of understanding -low level thinking) **shall guard your hearts and your minds in Christ Jesus**. Finally brethren, whatever is true, whatever is honorable, whatever is right, whatever is pure, whatever is lovely, whatever is of good repute, if there is any excellence and if anything worthy of praise, let your mind dwell on these things.

May God help us because, as we have no doubt found out, whatever is "inside" us will probably evidence itself through our mouth!

To know one's self is true; to strive with one's self is good; to conquer one's self in beautiful.

GRASPING GOD'S HAND

I was introduced to this illustration and was so impressed!

The hand illustration demonstrates God's sovereignty in our lives. It gives us the assurance of God's presence and His strength for our lives. By grasping God's hand and allowing Him to grasp ours, we have the ability to do what He asks us to do. Putting our hands in God's hands allows us to walk with him on a consistent basis.

Acts 11:"21 *"And the hand of the Lord was with them and a great number believed."*

Isaiah 41:10 *"Fear not, for I am with you, be not dismayed for I am your God. I will strengthen you, yes, I will help you, I will uphold you with My righteous right hand."*

What do the Scriptures mean? From time to time you hear another person say, "Someone had a hand in it." .....someone got involved. God wants to get involved in everything we do. He wants to make our lives work, make it enjoyable, and give real power to it.

There are many different types of Christians in the world. Some sparkle and shine and seem to overflow. Others are dull, listless and seem to be bearing up under the burdens of life as if they are like appliances that are not plugged in. Everything is there necessary to function but the power has not been appropriated. They are not "plugged in".

When we are born again.....the "old man or old nature" has not been annihilated, our spirit has been united with God's Spirit. We yield our soul activities, our mind, will, emotions to be Spirit controlled. We can choose to plug into the old nature or to the new nature.

Evidences of the Spirit-filled life:

Power -   Acts 1:8, We receive power after the Holy Ghost is come.

Love -   John 13:34,35, Love is a commandment, by this shall you be known as my disciples if you have love for one another.
1 Corinthians 13:47 Love is a fruit of the Spirit
Galatians 5:22 The fruit of the Spirit is love, joy, peace, patience, kindness, goodness, faithfulness, gentleness and self control.

How to live the Spirit controlled life

Confess: 1 John 1:9 If we confess our sins, He is faithful and righteous to forgive us and to cleanse us from all unrighteousness.

Obey: 1Peter 1:21 thru 23 You have in obedience purified your souls...and love one another...for you have been born again thru the living and abiding word of God.

Practice: Galatians 5:16-26 We walk not according to the flesh (our old nature, our mind, will, and emotions) but according to the Spirit (our spirit has been united with His Spirit-when we were born again). We make a choice!

THUMB - Represents the sovereignty of God
FIRST FINGER - Life
MIDDLE FINGER -Holy Spirit
RING FINGER - The Word
LITTLE FINGER - Faith
SOVEREIGNTY OF GOD

The **THUMB** of the hand is needed for a strong grasp.

SOVEREIGNTY: We need to let God control our lives. He wants to direct us. God is in charge. He is omnipotent. He is everywhere (ubicquous). He held the sun for Joshua for 23 hours. He held back the Red Sea so the Children of Israel could cross. He knows how to care for us as well.

1st *Peter 5:6-7, tells us to "humble ourselves under the mighty hand of God that He might exalt us at the proper time, casting all of our anxiety (cares) upon Him , because He cares for us."*

Anything that concerns us, concerns Him.

Jeremiah 1:6:9 records that God asked Jeremiah to do a job for Him that Jeremiah did not want to do. He said *"Lord God! Behold I cannot speak; for I am a youth."* But the Lord said to Jeremiah, *"Do not say that I am a youth; for you shall go to all to whom I send you."* It is important to go where the Lord sends. When He leads, He always empowers.

It is not you who speaks, but the Spirit of your Father who speaks in you. Matthew 10:20.

We are talking about the importance of the sovereignty of God. There is a story about Adoni-Bezek in the first chapter of Judges. When he would capture a country, he would bring back the King of that country to Bezek and cut off his thumbs and big toes. He did this to seventy kings.

There came a time that Judah took his warriors up to the land of Bezek and pursued and caught Adoni...and cut off his thumbs and big toes. Verse7 "Adoni said, 'seventy kings with their thumbs and their big toes cut off used to gather up scraps under my table; as I have done, so God has repaid me."

Can you imagine how difficult life would be without thumbs, such as holding utensils, cups, glasses, lots of activities in life. Thumbs are useful. Also in walking big toes gives us balance. This story is a good example of sowing and reaping!

But the Helper, the Holy Spirit, whom the Father will send in My name, He will teach you all things and bring to your remembrance all things that I have said. John 14:26

God is sovereign and He has a sovereign plan for each life!

LIFE – FIRST FINGER

We are responsible for our lives!

This has reference to our **FIRST FINGER** of our hand.

God's word teaches us how to live, love and forgive as we obey His commandments we are changed from glory to glory.

Jesus came to show us God's nature. He left, He sent the Holy Spirit. It is our responsibility to show the world the nature of Christ.

Every Christian is responsible to live a life that glorifies God and to be a real ambassador for Christ. God lives in us.

1 Corinthians 6:19: "Do you not know that you are the temple of God and that the Spirit of God dwells in you?" God wants to live His life through your life. By faith deny yourself, put off the old man and let Christ reign supreme. God will shape your life and make it worthwhile.

Acts 6:3 The disciples were looking for men to help them with the ministry. "*Therefore brethren, seek out from among you men with good reputations, full of the Holy Spirit and wisdom whom we may appoint over this business.*" As they sought for spiritual leaders they looked at the life of the individual. Our lives are like show windows. 2 Corinthian 3:2 states, "*you are our epistle written in our hearts, known and read by all men.*" People read us more clearly by our behavior than what they hear or by what we say. Our lives at home, at school, at play and in business speak clearly to the unbelieving world around us. Our lives bear witness to who/what we are.

Example: My hair dresser's husband is not a Christian and observes the neighbors who are church goers but their private lives do not measure up. Therefore, he declares that Christians are hypocrites!

Philippians 2:13-15 states, "*For it is God who works in you both to will and to do for His good pleasure. Do all things without murmuring and disputing that you may become blameless and harmless, children of God without fault in the midst of a crooked and perverse generation, among whom you shine as lights in the world*". We need to be beacon lights, bringing people safely to the harbor of salvation!

God demonstrates His power through a Spirit-controlled life. Allow the Holy Spirit to control your life.

LIFE IS A MIRROR AND WILL REFLECT BACK TO THE THINKER WHAT HE THINKS INTO IT.

HOLY SPIRIT – MIDDLE FINGER

(Our MIDDLE FINGER of our hand adds strength to our grasp)

Paul wrote in Eph 5:18 *"And do not be drunk with wine, but be filled with the Spirit"*. Each day that we are not filled with the Spirit, we are being cheated out of the blessings of God. Others, too, are being cheated by not seeing the fruit of the Spirit in your life. Every believer has the Holy Spirit, but the question is, "To what extent does the Spirit control your life?"

The Spirit-controlled life is obtained by confession of sin, obedience to Christ and walking in the Spirit, one step at a time. When you fall and fail, reach out your hand to God in confession. Confession simply means to agree with God regarding sin! God decides what is sin! The moment that you fall, confess it. God's hand is immediately there to put you back on your feet again.

Sin is "missing the mark".

Until you reach out to God in confession, you remain in your sins and you are the loser. Instead of having peace and joy in your heart, you are disillusioned, frustrated and defeated. However, if you learn to walk with God day by day, with your hand in His, you will know His anointing in a new and exciting way.

1 John 1:9 promises, *"If we confess our sins, He is faithful and just to forgive us our sins and to cleanse us from all unrighteousness"* When our lives are purified thru confession, the Holy Spirit will fill our lives and control them.

Paul wrote in Eph 5:18 *"Be filled with the Spirit"* God's command, therefore is to be filled with the Holy Spirit. Who is in control of your life right now? Actually, it is up to you. From Gal5:16 we learn if we *"walk in the Spirit, we will not fulfill the lust of the flesh"*

Again, God clearly reminds us that it is our duty to obey Him. Are you controlled by The Holy Spirit? Does He control your tongue, your eyes, and the other members of your body? Remember, we do not need more of the Holy Spirit, rather, He needs more of us!

John 14:16 in the amplified Bible states, *"And I will ask the Father and He will send you another Comforter (counselor, helper, intercessor, advocate, strengthener, and standby) that He may remain with you forever.*

We are born again by the Spirit of God. He gives us new life, prays for us, teaches us, seals us in Christ, assures us and He is our guide. He wants to make our life exciting day by day. Are we taking advantage of this resource?

You cannot drive a car without gasoline. It is just as foolish to try living the Christian life without the power and control of the indwelling Spirit.

Act 1 tells us that we will receive power after the Holy Spirit comes upon us. The first thing we need is power over our selves, the old nature.

The Holy Spirit is the one who day by day is making us more like Christ and He does it thru the Word of God and as we yield and are obedient, then we are changed from glory to glory. God is glorified as we are changed. Bearing fruit is a process, not an immediate response to salvation.

Our spirit is united with God's Spirit, however we wake up the next morning with our same old nature....

Rom 3:23 *"For all have sinned and come short of the glory (nature) of God.*

WORD –RING FINGER

The Ring Finger - relationship

Hebrews 4:12 ***"For the word of God is living and powerful and sharper than any two edged sword, piercing even to the division of the thoughts and intents of the heart."***

The more that we are in the Word, the more readily the Holy Spirit can speak to us, convict us, illuminate us and keep us on track. If we are to be effective Christians, we must gain a working knowledge of the Scriptures to share with others and also to guide our own lives.

The natural mind does not understand the word of God. However, as we abide (live) in Christ and His word becomes alive in our hearts, (understanding) then revelation for our own personal lives will be made known.

John 15:7 relates the mark of a disciple. Jesus said, *"If you abide (live) in my word and my Word abides (lives) in you. You can ask what you will."* Verse 8 states that we will bear much fruit.....fruit is the nature of Christ

God's word is a dynamic force in the Christian's life. Everyone must have some authority for why he believes what he believes. Our authority is the Word of God. The Bible. The greatest **attacks against authentic Christianity have always been centered in** either the person of Jesus or the authenticity of the Word of God.

We find in the religious world today that people use the Word mainly to prove a doctrine and not to practice. However, we must do more than read the Word, if we practice the Word of God, our natures will change.

FAITH – SMALL FINGER

The small finger - believing

I believe that God's utmost desire has been that His people would believe Him and obey Him.

Hebrews 11:6 states, *"But without faith it is impossible to please Him for he who comes to God must believe that He is, and that He is a re-warder of those who diligently seek him."*

God wants all of us to take Him at His word, to believe Him to do new things in our lives, to use us, to make our lives attractive, and to take over in areas of our lives that we have committed to Him.

Therefore, step out in faith in a new way. Faith is "trusting God completely." Take Him by the hand Trust Him for great things in your life.

Exercise your faith today, Right a wrong, straighten things out with others, make amends, ENDEAVOR TO LIVE WITHOUT

OFFENSE TOWARD OTHERS. Begin to witness to others, despite your fears. Take a step of faith.

Allow God in His sovereignty to control your life thru the power of the Holy Spirit by being prepared thru the Word of God and then by faith stepping out to allow Him to touch someone else's life through you.

The word "confidence" is taken from two words meaning "with faith". In other words, we put our confidence in God when we trust him to meet our needs and to use us in His service. Let us make the decision to believe God and obey Him.

Sow a thought....reap an act

Sow an act....reap a habit

Sow a habit.....reap a character

Sow a character...reap a destiny

THE END

Partakers of the Divine Nature

2 Peter 1:2-4: " Grace and peace be multiplied to you in the knowledge of God and of Jesus our Lord: Seeing that His divine power (*no power can resist it*) has granted to us everything pertaining to life **(happy life)** and godliness through the true knowledge of Him who called us by His own glory and excellence.

For by these He has granted to us His precious and magnificent promises (*Jews were distinguished in a very particular manner by promises which they received from God - to be their God, to protect, to provide, take to the promise land, etc-Paul is talking to Gentiles saying to them that God has made a valuable, precious, magnificent promise to them which came through a great price - the cross*) in order that by them you might become partakers of the divine nature (*the object of all of God's promises is to bring fallen man back to the "image of God". We have partaken of an earthly, sensual and devilish nature - the purpose of God is not to give us another "religion" but to give us a NEW NATURE*) having escaped the corruption that is in the world by lust."

LUST: - irregular, unreasonable, inordinate and impure desire. Lust is the source from which all the corruption which is in the world springs! Lust conceives and brings forth sin. Sin is finished or brought into act and then brings forth death. This destructive sin is to be rooted out and love to God and people to be implanted in its place. This is every Christian's privilege. God has promised to purify our hearts by faith. We can be delivered out of the hands of our enemies and even the thoughts of our hearts cleansed by God's Holy Spirit. This blessing may be expected by those who are continuing to escape from the corruption that is in the world and in themselves.

1 Peter 1:5-10: "Now for this very reason also, applying all diligence in your faith, supply (*this is a picture word that has reference to a Grecian dance - dancing with joined hands*) moral excellence (*so our faith that gives us hope is going to join hands and dance together with moral excellence - the courage and fortitude to stand up for what you believe. At an age when external controls have become weak, we must set our standards according to God's word. We must set them high, choose a higher path than that which the world travels. We must choose a more difficult goal. We must strive for moral excellence*) and in your moral excellence, knowledge; (*true, not false and not religious but a knowing that will bring wisdom*) and in your knowledge, self control (*a proper and limited use of all earthly enjoyments keeping every sense under proper restraint and never permitting the animal part to subjugate (rule) the rational*) and in your self control, perseverance (*patience; being constantly consistent in our Christian walk; bearing all trials and difficulties with an even balanced mind*) and in your perseverance, godliness (*a deep reverence, religious fear not only worshiping God but adoring, loving and magnifying Him in our hearts. This is necessary to salvation and it is rare among those who "profess" Christianity.*) and in your godliness, brotherly kindness (*the strongest attachment to Christ's flock (body) feeling each as a member of your own body.*) and in your brotherly kindness, Christian love. (*agape love-not based on feelings but a commitment to each other and to the will and purpose of God.*) For if these qualities are yours and are increasing, they render you neither useless nor unfruitful in the true knowledge of our Lord Jesus Christ. For he who lacks these qualities is blind (*he has willfully closed his eyes to the truth*) or short sighted, having forgotten his purification from his former sins. (*grieved the Holy Spirit by not showing forth the virtues (fruit) of Him who has called him into His marvelous light*) Therefore, brethren, be all the more diligent to make certain about His calling and choosing you; for as long as you PRACTICE these things, you will never stumble."

ONE OF THE GREATEST MIRACLES OF CREATION IS DISCOVERED IN THE FACT THAT AN INFINITE AND MIGHTY GOD FINDS GREAT PLEASURE AND SATISFACTION IN HIS TIMES OF FELLOWSHIP WITH US - YOU AND ME!!

Prayer

(notes taken from a Bible study)

WE ARE DISTRIBUTERS, NOT PRODUCERS. WE DO NOT HAVE TO PRODUCE ANYTHING....RECONCILIATION, DELIVERANCE, VICTORY, ETC....BUT RATHER WE DISTRIBUTE AS THE DISCIPLES DID WITH THE LOAVES AND FISHES.

OUR CALLING AND FUNCTION IS NOT TO REPLACE GOD BUT TO RELEASE HIM!

THIS LIBERATES US FROM INTIMIDATION AND EMBOLDENS US TO KNOW THAT:

THE PRODUCER WANTS TO DISTRIBUTE THROUGH US
THE INTERCESSOR WANTS TO INTERCEDE THROUGH US
THE MEDIATOR WANTS TO MEDIATE THROUGH US
THE REPRESENTATIVE WANTS TO RE-PRESENT THROUGH US
THE GO BETWEEN WANTS TO GO BETWEEN THROUGH US
THE VICTOR WANTS HIS VICTORY ENFORCED THROUGH US

GOD CONTINUES TO INCARNATE HIS REDEMPTIVE PURPOSE IN HUMAN LIVES.

WE DO NOT DEFEAT THE ENEMY, THE WORK IS ALREADY DONE

CHRIST NEEDS A HUMAN ON THE EARTH TO REPRESENT HIM. GOD 'S HUMAN WAS JESUS CHRIST.....JESUS'S HUMANS ARE US, THE CHURCH.

"AS THE FATHER HAS SENT ME, I ALSO SEND YOU." JOHN 20:21

A REPRESENTATIVE IS A "SENT ONE" AND "SENT ONES HAVE AUTHORITY.

WE ARE LITERALLY RE-DOING WHAT CHRIST DID, WE ARE RE-PRESENTING WHAT HE DID.

HE IS THE FOUNTAIN OF LIFE
JEREMIAH 2:13
JEREMIAH 17:13
BUT WE ARE THE DISPENSERS OF HIS LIVING WATER.

HE IS THE COMFORTING SHEPHERD'S STAFF {PSALMS 23:4}
HE ALLOWS US THE PRIVILEGE OF EXTENDING IT.

HE BORE OUR WEAKNESSES, HE IS ALSO STILL "TOUCHED WITH THE FEELINGS OF OUR INFIRMITIES.
HE WANTS TO TOUCH US WITH THE SAME COMPASSION FOR OTHERS.

THINK ABOUT IT:
THE GREAT HEALER HEALING THRU US
THE GREAT HIGH PRIEST "PRIESTING" THRU US'
THE GREAT LOVER, LOVING THRU US

PROTECTIVE BOUNDARIES CAN BE BUILT FOR OURSELVES AND OTHERS THROUGH PRAYER AND INTERCESSION

"WHY DOES GOD ALLOW EVIL THINGS TO HAPPEN IN THE WORLD"?

GOD WILL NEVER DECIDE A PERSON SHOULD BE RAPED OR ABUSED
HE WILL NEVER DESIRE THAT THE INNOCENT SUFFER
HE WILL NEVER MURDER, PILLAGE, CAUSE RACIAL GENOCIDE AND A THOUSAND OTHER THINGS

GOD GAVE ADAM AND HIS FAMILY CHOICES. ALL MADE THEIR OWN CHOICES OUT OF THEIR OWN SOULISH, CARNAL, EMOTIONAL THINKING AND FEELINGS.

THAT IS WHY WE PRAY.....TO GIVE OUR SPIRITS A CHANCE TO INFLUENCE CHOICES THAT WE SHOULD MAKE.

PRAYER IS IMPORTANT.....WE CAN COMMUNICATE WITH OUR CHRIST GIVEN SPIRITUAL NATURE AND NOT RESPOND TO OUR OWN HUMAN NATURE.

Spirit of a Bride

We were in a camp meeting at Wallow Lake....sometime in the '70's. I was listening to my friend, Shirley Miller tell about how she saw Jesus in a dream and how he looked at her with eyes full of love. I thought, "Lord, why don't I have experiences like this with you? I know that you love me, but I would like to know your love...not just by faith but experience!

I have always admired women who seem to have an insatiable hunger and desire to study and pray. This is the way I wanted to be.... but I was always so busy!

The next day Leon was ministering. He was talking about Adam and Eve and how they were "naked before each other and were not ashamed". He was explaining that this meant they were transparent in their relationship, they hid nothing from each other. I thought what a wonderful relationship that must have been...and then I began to contemplate of how thoughtful it was of God to plan this relationship when he created Adam and Eve. Then I thought, "God is also preparing a bride for Jesus---and I am a part of that bride". My heart began to pound inside of me as I began to consider myself as the bride of Christ! It was then that He showed me myself as a neglectful bride! Have you ever known of a wife in the natural who dotes on her house and her children and neglects her husband? There just doesn't seem to be enough time to even discuss the problems or the joys of the children or to even seek for his council and wisdom..

She makes the needed decisions alone. At the end of the day there is opportunity to be alone and to express to him words of love, appreciation, she is just too exhausted from her busy day, she gives him a "love pat" and goes to sleep, not even taking into consideration his needs. I reflected on the many times that I have gone to bed and then remembered that I had not prayed, or spent time in the word, but I had been very busy. I mean, I was a pastor's wife and there are millions of things to do and after all, "they are your children, Lord, and it is your work and everything that I have done, I've done it for you. You know that I love you, Lord"....and off to sleep!

It was at this time that I heard the words, "TO KNOW MY LOVE, YOU HAVE TO SPEND TIME WITH ME". I began to weep, I knew this was true, you cannot know anyone's love unless you spend time together! I know that I had been busy about many things. I have never appreciated hearing anyone putting Martha down because I always thought "someone must do the work". I loved the people and enjoyed my church family and my busy life! I cried out for the Lord to help me, to change my nature and give me a stronger desire to spend time with Him. He said, "you have a mother's heart, but I desire to give you the SPIRIT OF A BRIDE'. I had received a love call from my Lord! He wants me to learn to sat at His feet and adore Him. He wants me to seek for ways to please Him and He is willing to help me. He didn't tell me that my "mother's heart" was bad or wrong, only that I had my priorities mixed up.

He showed me that even though I had been a neglectful bride, he had been a faithful husband. He had promised to never leave me nor forsake me and he had waited patiently and longed for the times that I would find to spend with Him, even though, it was mostly when I had problems and I would turn to Him for help, but He was always there. HE IS SO FAITHFUL! He never turned me away.

Jesus and the Church are compared to a husband-wife relationship. We must have an intimate relationship- a love relationship with Jesus. Matt. 7:21 talks about the end time and those who will stand before Him and say "have we not done many works in your name" but, He will say "depart from me, I never KNEW you". This word "KNEW" comes from the same word as "Adam KNEW his wife and she conceived" - a love relationship. If we have been too busy for the love relationship, all of our works will be hay, wood and stubble and will be burned as rubbish on that great day.

As we spend time with Jesus and know His heart and seek to please Him, we will know when to work and what to do. You know, Jesus wasn't bothered at Martha about what she was doing, it was her timing! He had not asked her to prepare food for Him, he wasn't hungry. This was Martha's idea. There is a time to serve and a time to sit at His feet. If we sit at His feet first, He will let us know when we should serve!

It has been hard to change my nature and to learn to sit instead of go, but He is still patiently and lovingly helping me and more and more I am knowing the importance of spending time - quality time with my Beloved!

Loved by God

Recently, Leon and I were in the Sunday morning service at our local church. During the worship time, I was standing with my arms raised and telling Jesus how much I love and appreciate Him. I was thanking Him for salvation, for my life, for His love, His provision, His care, for my family, and feeling that words were just not adequate to express my feelings....but He knew my heart. I became quiet and at that time, I feel that He began to speak to me! These words came to me, "I was there when you were born, I was with you when you took your first breath. I have loved you all of your life." Oh My! How sweet that was!

At that time, I remembered a happening many years ago. Leon and I were very young and were pastors at our home church in Harrisburg, Oregon. Sometimes, even pastor's wives can become hurt and discouraged. At the close of a meeting, I walked up for prayer. Brother Al Farrah, a very special man of God, usually soft spoken, walked over to pray for me and with forceful words began to speak. "God has not called you and chosen you, even from your mother's womb that you should fall by the wayside. God says, 'I have a plan for your life. I cannot reveal to you the plans I have for you for your heart would faint....'"

Another time, Brother Don Krider was with us and he called me up to pray for me. He said, "Do you know how valuable and important you are to your husband and ministry?" I replied, "No."

He said that God was knitting our hearts together as one and when time and miles separate us, and that will happen, we would still be as one. At that time, the only miles that separated us were when we went to work! However, God surely knew our future and He had it planned.

I have thought that surely my heart would have fainted...this is true. Little did we know what the future held for us. We have had the privilege to go many places in the world. We have touched lives in different cultures and have been touched by them! We have loved and been loved by so many different people. God has taken us to the Philippine Islands, countries in Africa, India, China, Hong Kong, Malaysia, Venezuela, Cambodia, Mexico and Canada. However, it seems the intensity of time and effort has been focused toward the Philippine Islands and in Africa.

On our first trip to West Africa, on the way to the airport for our return home. one of the young pastors made a statement, "Mama and Papa, you are true missionaries. You did not spend your time in the hotels but you ate our food, slept in our beds and touched our lives."

I am still amazed that God has chosen us to go to these nations and love and be loved by people of these nations. It has been a GOD THING. We did not look for it or plan it, it just happened, one step, one day at a time. Leon is an excellent teacher and we have had the privilege of teaching, sharing, and being an expression of God's love in our travels.

I give thanks to you, Jesus, for helping us to fulfill your plans for our lives. Life is good!

Here is my love song to Jesus. I put it together about 30 years ago, walking down a dirt road in Fox, Oregon when visiting our son, Ric and wife, Vickie.

I love you. Jesus, more and more every day
I love you, Jesus, in a special way
Time spend with you is so precious indeed
Time spent with you, satisfies my needs.
I thank you, Jesus, for being so faithful

While carelessly I went my own way
Little did I know all the treasures untold
Could all be mine by spending time with you
You are my Savior, You're my dearest friend
You are my beloved, on you I depend
You give me council, You direct my days
I love you, Jesus, teach me to please you.

This is a prayer that Leon's mother prayed for him:

Let us bring forth your word, Lord, with demonstration and power
For great is the need, Lord, and late is the hour
Give a mouth and wisdom, no one can gainsay
Make a way, Lord where there seemeth no way
Seeking thy will, Lord, forsaking our own
Lead us to heights Lord, that we've never known
And deeper depths Lord, we earnestly pray, Make a way Lord, where there seemeth no way
Open the doors Lord, that no one can close
Reveal the secrets that no one knows
And our all on the altar, we surely will lay
Make a way, Lord, where there seemeth no way
Make a way Lord, where there seemeth no way
Give us faith to step out on your promise each day
Knowing you will provide Lord, protect all the way
Make a way Lord, where there seemeth no way

Commercialism of Christmas

I wrote this for an assignment in a college class.

The commercialism of Christmas has become increasingly difficult for families in today's economy. Too often my husband and I have gone into debt (and I am sure others have done the same) and then struggled during the year to pay off the debt-just to do it again- and why? Is it because of the pressures of society or is it due to religious convictions? This has caused me to take a serious look into the practice of this celebration to determine exactly how important it is in my own life and to look for ways to lessen some pressure.

Christmas is a celebration of the birth of Jesus! Right? What does the tree, the holly, the mistletoe, Santa Clause, the reindeer, card giving - all of these things that have become so traditional and ingrained in our society, have to do with Jesus being born? And since no one really knows the actual date of His birth, why do we celebrate it on December 25th? Where did all of these customs originate?

Let's start with the date. "Christmas originated at the time when the "Cult of the Sun" was particularly strong at Rome. December 25th was the date of the Solstice - a worship of the sun and the time the sun began its return to the northern skies. Pagan devotees of Mithra celebrated the birthday of the invincible sun" on December 25th 274A.D. Aurelian had proclaimed the "Sun-God Principle" and built a temple to him (New Catholic Encyclopedia #3, page 656).

The Encyclopedia Britannica, Volume #5, Page 704-705 states, "December 25th was the date of a pagan festival in Rome chosen in 274 A.D. by Aurelian as the birthday of the conquered sun and was established as a date for the commemoration of Christ by the Roman Church around 356 A.D. It was a time of merry making and exchanging of presents.

In the United States, traditional customs were at first suppressed (as in England under the Commonwealth), because of the Puritans' objection to them as Pagan origin, but since the middle of the 19th century, the celebrations have become increasingly popular and commercialized."

The Two Babylons, Pages 87-90 states, "The beginning of the Kingdom of Babylon was mentioned as early in the scriptures as Genesis 11, with Nimrod as the king. The beginning of the pagan worship can be traced to this time and was worshiped under the names of 'Bel and Bal'. Nimrod was deified especially after his death, being proclaimed as the 'promised one', who would come and was destined to 'bruise the serpent's head'. He was proclaimed the 'Messiah' or 'promised one'. The mother of the child became an object of worship and was raised to divinity as well as her son. The day of Jesus' birth cannot be determined and in the Christian Church no such festival as Christmas was ever heard of until the 3rd century. However, long before the birth of Jesus, December 25th was celebrated among the heathen nations (Idol worshipers) and it was in honor of the birth of the 'Son of the Babylonian Queen of heaven' (Nimrod). The same festival was adopted by the Roman Church giving it only the name of Christ Jesus!"

THE TREE: "The Christmas tree now so common among us was equally common in Pagan Rome many years before Christ. The mother of the Sun-god was mystically said to have changed into a tree and when in this state to have brought forth her divine son. This entirely accounts for the putting of the Yule Log into the fire on Christmas Eve, and the appearance of the Christmas Tree the next morning. The tree is Nimrod - the slain god come to life again." (Two Babylons, Page 97-98)

MISTLETOE: "The mistletoe bough was a representation of Nimrod, called the Messiah, 'The Man, The Branch' and was regarded as a divine branch that came from heaven, and grew upon a tree that sprang out of the earth. Heaven and earth were joined together and the mistletoe became the token of divine reconciliation to man, the kiss being the well-known token of pardon and reconciliation." (The Two Babylons, page 97).

SANTA CLAUSE: "Santa Clause (St. Nicholas) served as a bishop in Asia Minor in the 300's A.D. He was famous for his generosity. He was believed to bring gifts to children on the eve of his feast day, December 6th. Gradually, he became accepted as a giver of gifts at Christmas time. This belief that Santa enters the house through the chimney developed from an old Norse legend. The Norse believed that the goddess, Hertha appeared in the fireplace and brought good luck to the home. In 1822 Clement C. Moore, an American minister and poet first described Santa's suit and his sleigh pulled by reindeer in his famous poem, "Twas the Night Before Christmas."" (The Two Babylons, Page 97)

CHRISTMAS CARDS: Christmas cards were not exchanged until recent times. The first card designed especially to be sold was created in 1843.

Is it possible that the ancient Romans, who had accepted Christianity, were really sick of the pagan festivals? Wanting desperately to promote changes in their practices and customs of the day, yet realizing the difficulties that confronted them in remolding an entire Nation, they substituted Christ in the place of the "birth of the sun" (Nimrod) and Mary replaced Nimrod's mother. This was the beginning of the worship of Mary. Was this possibly an effort to offset or counter the pagan worship? The answer is, Yes! It is very possible that these were truly believers of Christ.....but look what has happened. The rituals unrelated to Christ are still with us today, and every year gain momentum in society. Many celebrate Christmas who do not believe in Jesus.

It is now as with the ancient pagans - a day of drinking, revelry and exchanging of gifts. There is more emphasis put on the tree, the mistletoe, and the mystical fat man in the red suit, who mysteriously appears on December 24ᵗʰ with many gifts and then with a "ho-ho-ho' flies out of sight, only to be honored again the next year. He has rapidly replaced the true Giver of good gifts, who is with us every day and never leaves us.

The presented information leaves little doubt that the pressure of Christmas should be from society only! There is no commandment from Christ that we celebrate His birthday. If we do choose to give honor to Him on a special day, let us not cheat Him by placing Him in a corner and throwing Him a tidbit of occasional recognition. Instead, let us lay aside the tree, the yule log, the mistletoe and Santa Clause. Let us remember that God came to us in the form of a new born baby. Let us give Christ all of the honor, as the Giver of good gifts, into our lives and truly celebrate Him when we meet together with our families and friends.

I believe, if the commercialism of Christmas is to be lessened, it must begin with concerned Christian families. We cannot expect the society which is motivated by the business community, to lessen the pressure. I encourage all Christians to take a serious look at the history of the popular, traditional celebration, and take some positive steps toward change.

Coming Short of God's Glory

Last year we were in the Philippines, someone quoted the scripture **"For all have sinned and come short of the glory of God." Romans 3:23** I allowed myself to meditate upon this and thought, "What, exactly, have we come short of?" I have always thought of the "glory of God" as a nebulas out-of-reach splendor, majesty, or power that would never be attainable to us as mortals. I checked out the word "glory" with my Strong's concordance and found this word "glory" refers to a person's nature, character, soul, personality. (Strong's 1391) Therefore, the thing that we find ourselves short of is the nature and character of God!

My mind went to Exodus 33:13.....Moses knew and had experienced God's power in many different ways but in verse 13, Moses, desired to KNOW God, to know His ways. In verse 18 Moses said, "I pray Thee, show me thy glory." (Strong's 3519) This also refers to the soul, the personality. Reading chapter 34, God passed by Moses and M**oses saw the nature of God!** He saw that God was **compassionate and gracious** (merciful) and **slow to anger** (self control of sudden temper). He saw that God was **abounding in loving kindness** (always ready to bestow benefit of love, favor, mercy and grace to us!) He saw that God was **Truth** (faithful and trustworthy)! He saw that God **keeps** (guards, protects, maintains) **loving kindness**. He also found that God **forgives iniquities.** This refers to depraved actions, even a person whom society would consider hopelessly bad, an incorrigible criminal, God can forgive and work a change within that person! God also **forgives transgressions** (willful deviations from the paths of righteousness) and He also **forgives sin** (habitual sin...drugs, alcohol, lust, pornography, etc.) THIS IS OUR GOD! ISN'T HE A GREAT GOD? Not only is He all powerful, the creator of the universe, but He is also a God with feelings for you and me!

I followed through to St. John 17:22; the prayer that Jesus prayed for His disciples that they might be one. **"And the glory which Thou has given Me I have given to them that they may be one, just as We are one."** Jesus came to the earth to show us God's nature and character. We can look at Jesus and know God. Now, Jesus says that the glory which the Father had given to Him, He is giving to us, in order that we might be one, so that the world might believe! The only way the church world will ever become united is if we take on God's nature and character. Jesus will be glorified as we are changed! The world cannot see our love for God, but they can see if we have love for each other! Doctrines will never unite the Christian believers. Doctrines will unite some and divide from others.

We have heard the expression: "Keep your eyes on Jesus, if you look at people (Christian people) they will disappoint you because people are inclined to walk after their own desires and understanding (the Bible refers to this as walking after the flesh)." However, Paul encouraged others to imitate him. He said that he had not reached perfection (spiritual maturity) but this was his goal. People have a right to look at us and watch our lives and they should see Jesus, his nature, attitude and behavior. Our goal should be to attain to spiritual maturity as we are being changed daily from glory to glory! Our behavior, actions, and reactions are based on our attitudes. The true test of spiritual maturity will come under pressure...it is not only our actions but our reactions to situations that tell on us!

HOW DO WE GET THIS "CHRIST-LIKE NATURE"? Is it a magical mystical thing that "zaps" us and we are suddenly changed? **NO!** 1 Peter 1:23 tells us that we have been "born again" of an incorruptible seed (divine sperm). God's Spirit has been united with our spirit- not our soul- and this is through faith, not feeling. It does not necessarily involve our emotions, even though many times it does. Salvation is an act of FAITH.

However, being filled with the Holy Spirit is an experience and involves our five senses, our emotions. Act 1:8 tells us that we will receive power after we have received the Holy Spirit and the first thing we need power over is our own selves, our wills, emotions, our choices. The Holy Spirit becomes our battering ram on the inside of us, knocking down strong holds in our old nature. Our old nature has been programmed by this world, depending on our home life, education, social status, environment, self concept, etc..... and this behavior, thoughts, reaction patterns are still very much a part of us even after we have been born again.

Romans 12:2, tells us that we will be changed (transformed) by the renewing of our minds. God takes us and changes us into a person for His use and purpose. He will take all that we are and mold us into His image, keeping the good and eliminating all that He cannot use.

We must CHOOSE to **practice** the nature of God. 11 Peter 1:4-10 tells us that we become partakers of His divine nature by **practicing** the word of God. It is up to us to put new thoughts and directions in control and we have the Holy Spirit to help us do that. We can choose how we react to difficult situations.

1. We yield our senses (mind, will, emotions) to the Holy Spirit's control.
2. We obey His commands, not only when we FEEL like it, but when it is hard to do

a). Love - we are commanded to love one another, even if we do not FEEL love for an individual. It is not based on feelings (feelings are fickle and subject to change). If we show kindness, respect and value for that person, then we are loving. In Luke, chapter 6, Jesus says, if we only love those who love us, what is the big deal, even sinners do that. He said, the way you love your enemy is to "do good unto him". You are not required to "like" your enemy, you are required to "do good". Remember, Jesus' feelings did not want to go to the cross for us, He cried out three times "If it could be your will, let this cup pass from me" then as an act of obedience to the will of the Father, He said, "Nevertheless, not my will but Thy will be done". He stepped past His feelings and suffered the cross for you and me.... while we were living in sin!

b). Forgive - we forgive in the same way, not by feelings but a choice to forgive. Even when our feelings are still experiencing the pain, we can choose to forgive a wrong that has been done to us! We pray, lay the offense at the altar of prayer. Forgive the person and ask God to forgive them, also. The next time you see that person, even though you remember the wrong, and feelings rise to the surface, you take charge of your behavior and behave as though the wrong never happened! **Forgiveness is perhaps the hardest of all Christian accomplishments** but the rewards are also the greatest! Your feelings will line up with your choice as you continue to practice forgiveness!

The only access Satan has to us is through our feelings, our soul senses! He cannot touch our spirit because our spirit has been united with God, but he can sure play havoc with our soul. He uses our feelings so successfully to keep us from accomplishing God's will, God's best for our lives. Our actions and emotions are based on our attitudes and are affected directly by our senses. This is the battleground of the spirit world. We must choose to obey God's will for us. The choice to live our lives with our feelings in control is a sad commentary....there is a better way! God's way!

3. Learn to communicate with and listen to the Holy Spirit

Don't look for "quick fixes". Practice the word of God until it becomes a part of your nature. That is how habits are formed and that is how we will become changed! It will be awkward and unnatural to "put aside our old nature" and to "be transformed by the renewing of our minds" but, it can happen.

Examples:

1. When a baby learns to feed himself , he is pretty messy but with practice, it becomes no problem! When a baby is learning to walk, he falls down many times, but soon is "off and running". A child is trained by repeating behavior over and over. We never stop creating habits in our lives...be it good or bad. As we develop in our

Christian behavior, we are constantly making choices. We must choose to practice His word.

2. Learning to play an instrument is pretty awkward at first and the sounds coming out of the instrument is anything by harmonious, but as you continue to practice, soon your hands will cooperate and it has become a part of your nature!

1 John 3:7 "Let no one deceive you, he who **practices** righteousness is righteous, he who **practices** sin is of the devil". Verse 22: "Whatever we ask we receive because we keep His commands and DO those things that are pleasing in His sight".

Commandments were never given to appease our five senses! We will not always feel like keeping His commands! His commandments were given to us for our benefit to change us, as we practice them, into the character and nature of our Lord Jesus.

We do not have to live void of feeling, but our feelings must line up with the word of God. As we practice His word our nature will change. 3rd John 1:1 "Do not imitate what is evil but what is good. The one who does good is of God."

It is God's action and interference in our lives that is designed to bring us to the desired relationship with Himself. There are some things that **WE** are required to "lay aside".

Ephesians 4:22: "lay aside your old self and be renewed in the spirit of your mind....and put on your new self which is in the likeness of God". verses 31 and 32 "Let all bitterness (harsh, long term disagreement)**, and wrath** (reaction to bitterness)**, and anger** (sudden anger, temper) **and clamor** (demands, arguing)**, and slander** (damages another's influence) **be put away from you, along with all malice** (active ill will)**. And be kind to one another, tender-hearted, forgiving each other, just as God in Christ also has forgiven you."**

God's desire, His ultimate purpose is to change us into His nature and to reveal His power through His people, the Church!

Revelations 22:11 "Let the one who does wrong still do wrong...the one who is filthy, still be filthy, let the one who is righteous still PRACTICE righteousness...let the one who

133

is holy still keep himself holy...verse 12...behold I am coming quickly...."

Whatever we are practicing when He returns, that is the way we will stand before Him!

The world is waiting for us to show them Jesus!

A Toast to a Preacher's Wife

Author unknown

To that true paragon, a preacher's good wife
The most versatile creature you'll ever meet in your life
She must never be slouchy, nor yet overdressed
She must never seem worried, nor cross, nor depressed
She must know how to sew and to wash and to cook
And must always be ready to teach any book
She must go with her husband where'er he may roam
And yet must always be found attending her home
She must be tactful and gracious to saint and sinner
And never refuse to serve a church dinner
She must bring up her children to please all the flock
And attend all the meetings at the stroke of a clock
She must be witty and happy and ready for larks
But never offend by her clever remarks
She must know all the answers, yet be without bias
Just pious enough, but never too pious
She must know how to deal with the cranky and cross
The timid and shy and big would be "boss"
She must be a helpmeet for the man she has wed
A boost for the dark hours or a cure for swell'd head
Here is to the elect lady, the preacher's wife
You may meet a great many as you travel thru life
And tho' often heart-weary and often depressed
With faith and with courage their souls have been blessed
They march with heads high and banners unfurled
They are the happiest women in all of God's world

Spiritual Maturity

STUDY ABOUT THE FRUIT

A short time ago, I was reading in Matthew 24 when my attention focused on verse 24, *"In the last days false prophets will arise and will deceive many ... and if possible, even the elect. "* I thought to myself, "How can this be?" I read the verse again and the Holy Spirit began to speak into my mind. In the last days, the false church will so closely resemble the true church with the gifts, showing signs and wonders that people will flock to the spectacular and will be deceived. He said, "I *never said that you would know them by their gifts, abilities nor by signs and wonders but by their fruit"* (Matthew 7:15-20).

Spiritual gifts in a person's life will not produce and are not evidence of maturity or spirituality. God gives gifts to whomever He wills. New converts can exercise gifts. Carnal people can exercise gifts. The Corinthian church had all of the gifts functioning and yet Paul said to them, *"You are carnal, filled with envying, fighting and divisions."* Gifts are given freely by God and we do not have to work for them. We are told to desire them. Gifts and talents have a special place, they are tools of ministry. The more that we depend on our gifts and talents for ministry, the less time we will spend in prayer and God's Word.

I had a desire to look into the "fruit of the Spirit" as in Galatians 5:22. We are so prone to focus in on the blessings, gifts and the benefits. But if we have a desire for this Spirit of the Bride, we are to turn our eyes toward the *Giver*, our Beloved. Spending time with *Jesus* will produce godly character in us.

We are to be a planting in the house of the Lord. (Ps 92:13)
We will continue to bear fruit even in our old age.
(Ps. 92:14)
Fruit grows only in good ground. (Matt 13:8)
Fruit is a product of heavenly wisdom:
1. Must have contact with living water. (Ps. 1:3)
2. Spiritual receptivity (good ground). (Matt 13:23)
3. Death of the old life. (Jn 12:24)
4. Chastening-Pruning. (Jn 15:2)
5. Abide in Christ. (Jn 15:21)

1 believe that God's ultimate purpose is to reveal His nature through His people, and we are changed as we spend time in the presence of a Holy God.

"Now the works of the flesh are evident which are: immorality, impurity, sensuality, idolatry, sorcery, enmities, strife, jealousy, outbursts of anger, disputes, dissensions, factions, envying, drunkenness, carousing and things like these of which I forewarn you just as I have forewarned you that those who practice such things shall not inherit the kingdom of God" (Galatians. 5:19-21).

"But the fruit of the Spirit is love, joy, peace, patience, kindness, goodness, faithfulness, gentleness, self-control, against such things there is no law" (Galatians. 5:22).

Fruit is a product of the Christian experience, of a new and divine life implanted in the believer from the indwelling Spirit. As we live in the Spirit, we receive our spiritual life from this indwelling Spirit and it is natural that we bear fruit.
1. This fruit is for others to pick.
2. Fruit is singular. This shows that all of the elements of character are in unity, making for a well rounded and complete Christian life.

Upward To God—A Direct Connection To God

LOVE: This speaks not of the human love that is based on feelings but on God's Agape love which is based on an act of obedience to the will of God in your life, apart from feelings. "If you *love Me you will keep my commandments.*" Not that you will always feel like keeping His commandments, but you do them because it is the will of God for you. You have an intense desire to please God. This love gives energy to faith. For example, you love those whom you don't like by doing good to them. His commandments were never given to appease the flesh, but to change us into His likeness.

JOY: This joy is inwardly and spiritually based and is not dependant on the situation around you. *"Thou has put gladness in my heart, more than when new wine and grain abounds" (Ps. 4:7).* This joy is not dependent on what you have or don't have. This joy arises from a sense of God's mercy communicated to your soul that your iniquities (sins) have been pardoned and a surety that God loves you.

PEACE: This is not speaking of peace with God because we have justification (as though we never sinned). This speaks of the tranquility of your mind based on having a right relationship to God. It speaks of a binding together through the cross. You and God-through the cross of Jesus. This kind of peace will take care of those "terrors by night". How many of you have problems with thoughts at night? You lay on your bed and sleep won't come and your mind, your thoughts torment you. You worry, worry, worry.... This peace quiets the dreadful foreboding, the fears, the alarms.

These three, *love, joy, peace* are developed due to an upward communication--a vertical flow of communication between you and your beloved, *Jesus.*

Outward To Others--Your Expression Toward Others horizontally.

LONG SUFFERING: (Patience) This speaks of a steadfastness of the soul (5 senses: mind, will and emotions) to endure under impulse and temptation. You can be treated wrongly or tacky without thoughts of revenge. Bearing with the frailties and short comings of others and being able to bear up through the difficulties of life submitting to and deriving benefit from every situation.

GOODNESS: That quality in a person who is ruled by and aims toward the quality of moral worth. The perpetual desire to abstain from every appearance of evil and to do good to the bodies and souls of people to our utmost ability.

KINDNESS: (gentleness) A kindness that should pervade and penetrate our whole nature mellowing in it all that is harsh and severe. Gentleness is a very rare grace, often found wanting in many who have a considerable share of Christian excellence and abilities to minister the gifts. A good education and polished manners, when brought under the influence of the grace of God will bring out this grace with great effect. Gentleness is never rude with an attitude of vengeance. There is never an excuse to be rude, to refuse to speak or to acknowledge another's presence.

True friendship is a commodity that is really lacking in today's world. It has been said that if you have one or two *True* friends in a life time you are blessed and it is rare. We go through life with many acquaintances but seldom a *true* friend. If you have these qualities, you can *be a true friend.*

Inward To Self-Outward Character Development

GENTLENESS: (meekness) A gentle, meek spirit refers to that personality that is without complications. A benign personality; not harmful;. a mild personality; one that is indulgent toward the erring and the weak; a patient suffering of injuries without feeling of revenge; an even balance of tempers and passions. This is a person who is disciplined. *"He disciplines us for our good that we may share His holiness"* (Heb. 12:10). "All *discipline for the moment seems not to be joyful .... yet, to those who have been trained by it, afterwards it yields the peaceful fruit of righteousness."* (Heb. 12:11). This word "meek" does not reference one who is weak. It comes from the idea of "meeking" a horse; training a horse so its strength and abilities can be used for your purpose. Gentleness is the opposite of anger.

FAITH: (Faithfulness) This is a person who is trustworthy in performing promises. Fidelity. One who is conscientious in preserving what is committed into his trust either in business transactions or not betraying the secret of a friend or disappointing the confidence of an employer. Let faithfulness be produced in your lives as you are yielded to the Holy Spirit.

TEMPERANCE: (Self-control) This is possessing the power and having mastery over your behavior. It is keeping every sense under proper restraint and never permitting the animal part to subjugate (rule) over the rational. I Corinthians 7:9 speaks of having control over sexual desire. I Corinthians 9:25 refers to the control of an athlete over his body and its desires. You can have mastery over your own desires and impulses.

Character traits of the spirit are formed in you by degrees and under pressure. As you abide in Christ your character is transformed to be like the most lovely character of Jesus. Patience, kindness, goodness, gentleness, faithfulness and self control are thought of as "thermometer" fruits that ripen in time as the temperature rises. Joy and peace are "barometer" fruits that evidence themselves under pressure and if they are not in evidence, something is wrong. ***Love is*** both, a thermometer and barometer.

Just as there can be no salvation without the cross, there can be no fruit without the dying to self. Fruit is a product of maturity ... godly character. Gifts are free from God. Being gifted is not a certain sign of maturity. Satan can imitate the gifts, it is not possible to imitate the character (fruit) of the Spirit. I believe this is one reason that Jesus instructed us to "know those who labor among us". We need to know that they have developed fruit. Many recognized ministries are gifted. We should never follow a person because of the gifts. We must know them by their fruit! We can never "know" someone with whom we do not spend time. The importance of the local church can never be replaced by television for obvious reasons. You do not spend time with them in their natural setting apart from TV time. You do not know them. As we have stated before, gifts of the Spirit are tools for ministry and when gifts are continually used through a vessel that does not experience a changed nature and manifested character of Christ, this creates confusion in the church.

As the time of Christ's return draws near, may we not become deceived by the many signs, wonders and spectacular events that will be prevalent at the ending of this age. Even though at the time of this writing, the Church is experiencing exciting times, pray that our direction will be focused on the character of the ministries more than that of the gifts, that we not be deceived. The true, matured Church will have both, the gifts and the fruit of the Spirit functioning together in harmony, power and demonstration! "You *will know them by their fruit*" (Matt. 7:20).

THE END

I Remember Series
I Remember....A Dream that changed my thinking!

Leon and I were raised in a church that was quite legalistic...along with "outward appearance" emphasis were also taught that if you were not baptized in Jesus' Name and received the baptism of the Holy Spirit with the evidence of speaking in tongues....then you were not saved. Well! You can imagine what happened when we met Brother Welch and begin to have fellowship with him....and other people who did not share our particular doctrine! I, right away, began to talk to Brother Welch about baptism! When this attempt at conversion didn't work, I tried to keep Leon from getting so involved. (I was surprised to find that I was more indoctrinated in these views than Leon.)

When we were dropped and alienated by our original organization because of our fellowship with Brother Welch and the Full Gospel Fellowship, we were given the name of "compromiser", I was really confused and hurt.

One night I had a dream. I was walking down a familiar road and Jesus was walking with me. Jesus was sharing His heart with me, giving me revelation, instructions even sharing times, dates....so many things. Two men came up behind us and were arguing about the Godhead and baptism and I thought to myself, "Man, this is really opportune because I was sure that Jesus would just turn right around and reveal the truths of Himself to these men and let them know who He really is and how they should be baptized! Jesus just kept talking to me. It appeared he didn't even notice the argument that was taking place behind us. His attention was totally toward me and all that He wanted me to know. We came to crossroads and the two men turned and went their way, arguing. I interrupted the Lord, "Why didn't you reveal yourself and put a stop to the argument of those men." Jesus just looked at me with hurt in His eyes and said "I have so much that I want to share with you. This is what is important. They will know-the world will know who I am." I woke up and my heart was pounding. I literally jumped out of bed to get a pencil and paper so I could write down all that the Lord had been talking to me about......but the only thing that I could remember was the arguing going on behind me! What pain! What loss!

I told Leon the following morning about my dream and what had happened and told him that I would not fight with him anymore about the Full Gospel Fellowship and His relationship with Brother Welch. I said, "I do not understand it but for the Lord to come to me as He did, it must be important to Him for you to be involved in this Fellowship.

A few years ago at Brother Glen Richard's church in Olatha, Kansas, a man came up after church to visit. He asked me about our background and when I told him he said, "My! How did you ever get free from that?" I told him that the Lord did not change most of our doctrine....only our attitude. We still baptized in the name of Jesus. I thank God for the freedom from religious doctrinal bondage.

God did have a plan for us! Leon & Brother Welch walked together for 15 years and this vision was truly transferred into our hearts. St. John chapter 17 where Jesus says that we (Christians) should be one in unity and appreciation for one another. We do not have to believe the same in doctrines! One time Brother Gordon Lindsay questioned Brother Welch's wisdom of placing Leon in the Vice President position of the FGF because of their doctrinal differences using the scripture, "How can two walk together except they be agreed". Brother Welch gave a classic answer. He said, "We have agreed. We have agreed to walk together."

I am thankful that we are seeing the fulfillment of John 17 in the Full Gospel Fellowship as others are agreeing to walk together!

Vancouver B.C. Conference

Leon had attended a conference in Vancouver, B.C. and had met a group of people from the upper part of Canada. Clarence Vickers had invited him to come to visit and go "food" fishing with him.

After leaving Abe and Kathy Clausen, we headed on North toward Prince Rupert. I don't remember how long it took us... several days, and we stopped and visited a couple of churches. We finally arrived. I had never met any of these people and needless to say was somewhat nervous. Leon introduced me to Clarence, Rose and their young son, Warren. Leon and Clarence left the next morning on Clarence's boat "The Native Bride" for a few days of fishing.

I didn't know it, but Rose was even more anxious than I. Being left together - two strangers- me, white and she, native. They had not been saved for very long, however, the Lord was the one thing we had in common. We began to get acquainted and before the three days were over, a friendship was most certainly established!

After a few days, Leon and Clarence arrived on dock with a boat load of fish! Hundreds of salmon! I found out "man's work done", "woman's work begins"! They brought all of those salmon into Rose's kitchen to be canned! Then Leon and Clarence went to play basketball! I tried to explain that I do not cut off heads or gut fish, but they just laughed and told me that was "woman's work". I asked Rose if she had never heard of "equal rights". (smile) Randy & Wanda (Rose's sister) came over and gave me some pointers. We (Rose & I) worked until about 3 o'clock AM...slept about 4 hours and "hit it again" because we had to have them all canned by afternoon because we were going to Greenville (the village where Rose's family lives) for a high school graduation.

We made it and we were on our way! Now Greenville is a village about 90 miles from Terrace....on a logging road. When you get to the end of the road, you look across a River and there nestled at the base of a majestic mountain is Greenville. Clarence honked his horn, talked on his CB and someone promptly came over in a boat to take us to the village. There we met the Terry Stevens family. They welcomed us warmly. Rose's Mom cooked for us! We had fresh Halibut, fresh Salmon, Albacore (one of my favorites) with all the trimmings. They treated us so good.

I should mention here that when Rose & I were canning Salmon, I would throw the head in the garbage sack and Rose would dig around and choose heads that she set aside. Later when we cooked some salmon steaks, she put the heads in to cook. We found that they really liked the meat of the cheek of the salmon...that was a delicacy. We told them we would eat the steak and they could have the heads.

This was the first graduation held in their new high school. Leon and I found out that the government builds grade schools for the natives but if they wanted to go to high school they have to go to a boarding school hundreds of miles away. This was the first High School of their own,...so this was a joyous occasion.

This was the first of many visits to this village. Words would fail to try to explain the love and enjoyment that we have had in knowing and being loved by Clarence, Rose and the precious people in Greenville.

Two more things I should mention! I'll never forget the look on Clarence's face, the way his black eyes were laughing, when he & Leon came home from playing basketball. He put his arms around Leon's shoulders and said "I never knew a white man could be so much fun!" And # two - Clarence & Randy assured Leon that (after learning to cut off heads & to gut fish) I would make a good "squaw". I just needed some Indian discipline! (smile)

We have had fun times, serious times, spiritually uplifting times and most of all..the Lord brought special friendships into our lives that we still cherish to this day.

I Remember....Greenville Village

After our initial visit to Prince Rupert and our "bonding" experience, Leon and Clarence on the boat- fishing, and playing basketball-man's work. Rose and I, getting acquainted at home and then canning over 200 salmon in one night-woman's work. (smile) Leon & I returned home. However, this bonding time would be good for a life time. We kept in touch. Leon traveled to BC on several occasions for different meetings among the Natives. Rose & Clarence had successfully evangelized their villages taking in tapes, books, etc., for the people. Carroll Rowden, a young man from our church, accompanied Leon at one time, going with Clarence and other Christian brothers from Village to Village including some Islands, encouraging the new believers. Our son, Ric, went with Leon on one trip. They took a walk with Randy and Randy shot two moose! They were not near the village, about a mile upstream. They had to get the moose back to the village. Randy went for snowmobiles. They had to cut the moose up, put them on sleds and get them back to the village. They went for a walk about 3:00 pm, by the time they got this all done it was about 10:00 pm...all done in the dark! Wow! This was a major chore! Another memory!

However, I would like to focus in on MY next trip into Greenville! What an experience! On January 24, 1983, Ron & Joann Beeman, pastors from Asahka, Idaho, Chuck McCaul, a young man from our church in Harrisburg, Leon & I boarded a plane and headed toward Terrace, BC. As we approached Terrace, a report came that we may not be able to land because of the fog in the area. We began to breath prayers of "help" and right at the moment of turn around, the stewardess announced, "A wind came up and has cleared the ground at the airport and we will be able to land!"

Clarence met us, we loaded our luggage in his pickup and started our drive to Greenville; ninety miles on gravel road. When we reached the river it was about 10:30 PM and plenty dark! No lamppost! It was snowing, the river was frozen over and about 3 feet of snow on the top. It was cold and the wind blowing! We were supposed to walk across the river - 1/2 mile to the Village! I wasn't sure I was going to make it! I mean, when you are only 5 ft tall and you are plowing through 3 ft of snow......! I was coming in behind Joann and she got the "giggles" and kept falling down in the snow! Of course this helped in making a way for me! Joann's ability to laugh at this time really helped my own anxieties. We actually made it across the river, but when we arrived on land, the snow was above the house tops! Little tunnels had been kept cleared from house to house. All you could see is snow....and it continued to snow!. We were there for 10 days and spent our days and nights praying, teaching, having wonderful fellowship with each other. There were about 30 believers who were eager to study the word! We stayed in the home of Rose's parents and again, they treated us as Royalty. The ladies would bring in food and did we feast during our times of fellowship! Joann and I shared some special time with the women. Rose's parents told us about the Native's way of life in years past, about the "candle fish-ooligan-", the oil of this little fish is very valuable...and in years past, the fish was dried and burned as a candle. They told us how they had to grow their gardens because the growing season is so short...about how their ancestors survived the winters. We learned about traditions and what a tremendous strong hold these traditions have on the people. Our hearts were knit! Our emotions were stirred! Our love was strengthened! We were beginning to really know them! You can never truly love someone whom you do not know and do not spend time with. We prayed together, sang together, worshiped together, talked together, laughed together! I remember one night after the teaching, the women had put together some of their delicacies and Don started telling us Indian/White man jokes! About the first time he, Randy and Percy had killed a moose! I laughed until my sides hurt.

Today, as I write this little "I remember". I am remembering the Terry Stevens family, their home. I am remembering: Clarence, Rose, Randy, Wanda, John, Laveta, Percy, Darlene, Don, Karen, Elsie and her family, and many others! You are forever in my memory and in my heart!

I Remember.......Greenville Village in November

Do you remember our trip into Greenville, B.C. in January of '83? Well, Leon & I, being "quick learners", decided to beat the weather of the North Country and make our venture into the Village of Greenville earlier. So about the middle of November 1984, we boarded the plane once more looking forward to our time together with our friends in Greenville. Once again Clarence and Rose met us at the airport and we made our way to the Village.

The same as before, we arrived on the bank of Nass River about 10:30 pm- dark and cold. Clarence contacted friends in the village by CB and were told that an untimely freeze had happened and they were unable to bring the boat to get us.

We waited for some time and soon saw some lights crossing the river. I begged them "Please, let's just sit here in the pickup until morning". They said we could freeze. I was willing to take my chances there in preference to walking across that river in the dark. The water had not been frozen yet for 24 hours. In spite of my pleading, Randy Peters and a couple of other brothers from the village placed our luggage on a sled and away we went. The water had frozen during high tide and was as slippery as glass. It seemed I could hear it cracking underneath my feet! After slow progress we made it within 20-30 feet of the bank but the ice had broken and we could not reach shore. At one time, Rose & I were standing near each other and I think it was Clarence who told us to not stand close together...we needed to spread our weight out on the ice. Eventually some of the men of the village rolled a log down the bank and into the water for us to walk on to get to shore! We went to the Steven's home where we would be staying.

The next morning several friends came around to visit and as we sat around the table talking, they revealed to us their anxieties of the night before! They said the ice was not frozen more than 2 inches! It is an unwritten law in the village that they allow the ice to freeze for at least a week before they cross on it. Family and friends advised Randy and the others to not cross it so early. People were shaking their heads in awe...that we had actually crossed in safety. Surely the Lord's angels were moving us across the ice. All I could say is "Thank you, Jesus! You are so very faithful and trustworthy and I love you... and I just threw Him kisses".

We stayed for 2 weeks. We would have teaching morning and evening. In the afternoon the young men and Leon would go to the gymnasium and play basket ball or take walks, looking for moose. Leon loves it there...he gets to preach in his Levis, play basketball and go out looking for wild life. Randy told us about once, getting a Grizzle Bear caught in a trap... caught by his little toe, and it was so painful the bear just stayed there. In the afternoons, Rose & I took some walks, had some good visits with the other ladies in the village, and Rose's mom taught me to knit socks. (When I went home, I went on a knitting socks binge and I think I knit wool socks for about everyone!)

I wasn't too worried about getting out of there by now because that river has now had 2 weeks of freeze so my bravery was on the rise! Could you believe? The night before we were to leave, a high tide came in and broke the ice into pieces. Helicopters were air lifting the students across the river, but they were not allowed to take anyone but students. Okay! What to do?

We put our luggage in a boat and pulled it (the ground was covered with snow) to the river bank. We walked out on the first piece of ice, wedged the boat between that ice and the next piece of ice and used the boat to cross. We did that about six/eight times until we finally made it across. I remember the last piece of ice that we were standing on. There were six of us on the ice and the piece was only about 15/20 feet around and you could feel it tipping as we moved around, so we were very careful of our movements.

This was a great time to be there, in spite of the difficulties. It certainly increased our "bonding" with the wonderful family of

Greenville! I believe it was at this time that Elsie was set free from horrible depression.

As we remember these times in Greenville, BC, I am praying for another stirring of the Holy Spirit in the lives there. As we look around us and observe the season of the Spirit, the most urgent activity in our lives should be to prepare for the soon coming of the Lord Jesus. It is our desire to see every face that we ministered to in Glory on that Great Day!

I Remember...First Trip to the Philippines

I remember our first trip to the Philippine Islands! Leon said that when he received a letter from Pastor "Bonie" Simbran expressing the need for teachers, it was as though a hand reached out and took hold of his heart. Pastor Bonie wrote to Leon that the pastors attend a two year Bible School, but they need a teaching of deeper depths into the Word of God. Someone had given him Leon's name as a good teacher

Now, I had real mixed feelings about this. I had been to Mexico and Canada but there is a lot of water between Oregon and the Philippines! I wanted to go and I didn't want to go! Have you ever been there?

During the camp meeting at Lost Creek Camp, several words were given to us to confirm that we should answer the call to the Philippines. One of the words was that "the direction of the Full Gospel Fellowship would be changed from this time".

We spent time in Terry, Mt with Bob & Jeanne Strobel and Leon invited them to accompany us to the Philippines.

As time drew near for us to board the plane and cross the water, in November, 1983, I became more nervous. I entertained thoughts of never seeing my children, grandchildren or "my stuff" again. The night before leaving, we were in Puyallup, Washington and Darrel Buck gave me a word, "When your feet touch the soil of the Philippine Islands, your love and compassion for the people will overcome your fears!"

Our flight was due into Manila somewhere around midnight, with the domestic flight out again around 4:00 am (can't remember exactly). Anyway, we thought we would save the expense of a hotel room and just go directly to the domestic airport and wait there. Can you imagine our dilemma, when the taxi dropped us there and the airport was closed?! There we sat atop our luggage on the sidewalk for about 4 hours (in the dark). We had been up for 24 hours and we were tired! Finally, the airport opened and we were able to board the plane for Zamboanga. Day was just dawning as we descended the plank at our destination. A lovely young lady approached me and asked, "Are you Sister Willis?" and she put a lovely lei around my neck as she exclaimed "Hallelujah"...and it was true, the love and compassion that I have had for the Filipino people have overcome my fears.

I Remember...
First trip to the Philippine Islands #2

The year was 1983, Bob & Jeanne Strobel, Leon and I arrived in Zamboanga, Philippines just as it was dawning. We were met by Brother & Sister Simbran. They took us to a hotel for some very welcomed rest. We left for Ipil about 4:00 AM the next morning. From that time for the next 6 weeks, I was in total cultural shock!

Ipil was less than 100 miles away. It took us about 4 hours to drive there. We passed little grass huts, I asked if people lived there. Brother Simbran looked at me as though he didn't know what I meant. We passed many small barangays (small communities), a caribou pulling a cart with a young girl taking her laundry to the river to wash it. We slowed as we would pass through the barangay for the pigs, chickens, goats that were in the roads.

When we arrived, they cut a green coconut for us to drink the water from the coconut. We had been instructed by the doctor before leaving home that we should only drink water that had been boiled, eat only vegetables that were cooked. Finally our well lain plans were reality. I was actually in the Philippine Islands!

Around 100 pastors and their wives had gathered together for days of teaching and nightly crusades. As different ones gathered around to greet us and tell us their names, I thought, "How am I ever going to remember who is whom? They all look the same with dark (beautiful) skin, dark hair and brown/black eyes."

The weather was so hot! We aired up our air mattresses, stretched out our mosquito nets and prepared ourselves for ministry. It would cool down enough to sleep around 2 O'clock AM. The Filipinos days began at 3:30 AM. We would hear the voices begin to pray and sing and their first service was held at 5:00. We got up and around by 6:00 and our first service was at 8:30 AM. There was a short break, then another session at 10:30. Lunch at 12:00. We would be invited to a home for lunch, when we arrived, there would be around 100 Filipinos waiting for us and they would ask for some worship and a word before eating. The afternoon services was scheduled for 2:30 PM and a crusade in the evening.

One afternoon, Leon saw a young pastor leaning up against a tree and holding, what Leon thought was a bible. Leon asked him what translation of bible that he was using. He said, "This is not a bible, it is my notes. I do not own a Bible." We discovered that 90% of the pastors do not own Bibles. They will pass a Bible from one to the other and make notes from which to preach. Leon's heart cried. He purposed that one of our first projects when we returned home would be to send Bibles to the pastors in the Philippines!

We stayed in Ipil for 10 days. We became acquainted with the Filipino people. I visited with the women and discovered they are no different from me. They love their children, are concerned for their families. We shared with one another, prayed together and laughed together.

The women in the Philippines do not have any of the conveniences that we are accustomed to. They cook their meal over open fires outside. Only 2 places had refrigeration, so they had to go to market everyday in order to prepare food for the group. Bathroom facilities were probably the most difficult thing for Jeanne and me to cope with. The people did not have much in the way of comfort, but they gave us their very best!

We had one day without meetings and they took us to the beach. I had never experienced such warm water in an ocean...it was as warm as bath water. Jeanne & I picked up hundreds of shells. When we left Ipil for other parts of the Islands, we took them with us and Leon & Bob complained every time they had to carry them! We went to Liloy, Dipolog City and Midsayap. We met many pastors and wives who are giving their lives to minister the gospel in the Philippines. I had never known the kind of dedication that we met among some of the pastors here. They were well educated people with abilities to care for their families in the secular work force and yet God had called them to pioneer churches and they were sacrificing in many ways in order to do this.

We had never experience the kind of spiritual hunger that would cause families to walk for days to come to one service. In each place that we went, they came, they slept on benches, on the floor, they stayed as long as we stayed. We were in from 4 to 5 services a day. They wanted to be taught from the Word of God! They never tired of praising and worshiping! They were so excited and honored to be called of God to preach the gospel.

Our hearts were so touched by the Filipinos. We went to preach, teach and to be a blessing but we left feeling that we had learned a lot and were the ones who were blessed.

I Remember...Philippines 1998

James, Leon and I arrived in Manila about 5:30 am, February 13th. (It was already 85 degrees and the sun not up yet!). It was good to see Bob and Jeanne's smiling faces! We went to their place and James gave Leon and me "promised" haircuts! Bob and Leon began their "non-stop" talking! There was much excitement in the air and anticipation, looking forward to the next thirty days. Jeanne got busy confirming our tickets and scheduled air flights into the planned cities. James left about 4:30 for Davao where he was meeting with Domy and Nellie. He had brought a 16 millimeter projector and screen to be used in the mountains for evangelism.

Since the next day was Saturday, February 14th, plans had been made for a 10:00 am teaching, lunch, and a 2:00 marriage seminar. This was a good day with the church in Manila. Bob and Jeanne have been serving as Senior pastors here for about two years. Dick Boshta from New Orleans was scheduled to meet us while we were in Manila, so we picked him up at the air port and went to Kentucky Fried Chicken for dinner.

Sunday morning we were with Bob and Jeanne again. Brother Dick shared his vision of being a "working net" to unreached peoples of the earth. He remarked that this is the year of the glory of the Lord to fill His temple and the release of that glory! We are to be a part of that great completion. IT IS HARVEST TIME! Leon ministered. The presence of the Lord was there as ministry went forth meeting the needs of the people. We traveled across Manila to another church for the afternoon. Praise and worship was exciting! This is a fairly new work and already the place is packed! Pastor Bon and his wife, Ching are precious people. The Lord was faithful again and much ministry took place. Even at the end of the service, people could hardly stop praising, dancing, worshiping God. I remember Pastor Bon remarked "This is the beginning of something else!"

We had only been in the Philippines for two days.....two packed full days....this was only the beginning, we felt as though we had "hit the ground running"! Monday morning Bob, Leon and Dick had a meeting with some of the pastors in the area. Jeanne did laundry all day and we prepared our clothes and suitcases for the next three weeks.

On Tuesday, Bob, Jeanne, Leon and I left for Bacolod City (Brother Dick left for the USA). We were met by Pastor Ronnie Binas and his son and taken to the Regency Hotel to get settled, then we went to the dedication of a new church located near the sea shore. The congregation had been established for two years. It was a lovely bamboo structure with a gravel floor. (We left monies to put in a cement floor). We were served roast turkey and rice after the dedication. Pastor Ronnie and his wife, Dr. Salome Binas have around thirty-five churches which they have helped to establish.

The seminars were scheduled for Wednesday and Thursday. There were two sessions of the morning, two sessions in the afternoon and one evening meeting. Lunch was catered each day.

There were 130 pastors and workers registered for the seminars.

We left Saturday for Zamboanga, the southernmost part of Mindanao Island. Pastor Edman (senior pastor) and Pastor Kiko(assistant) met us and took us to guest cottages which are owned and had been provided for us by a member of their congregation. The rooms were built of bamboo, absolutely lovely! The landscape was well groomed and maintained. It was a comfortable, private place to rest. There was a birthday party planned in the afternoon, and a lady's meeting. I was scheduled to speak to the women , so after putting our things away, we went to the party. They had roast lechon (pig) with all the trimmings! They really know how to "throw a party"! Later in the evening, Pastor picked us up for dinner. They took us to a nice restaurant in town which is owned by a member of the church. Leon's voice was in pretty bad shape already. They brought him ginger tea! This gave him almost immediate relief! Praise the Lord!

The church has two services on Sunday morning. Bob ministered at 7:30 and Leon at 9:30. Bob ministered the evening service.

About 25 churches in Zamboanga were involved in the seminars. We understand that all of the Pentecostal churches participated plus many other denominations. Our days were very full! We would leave our rooms at 7:30 each morning and go to breakfast prepared for us by Ronald and Fely. Seminars scheduled for 8:30 until noon.... Lunch......afternoon meeting schedule from 2:00 until 5:00 with a one hour/thirty minuet break and evening service to begin at 6:30. A meal would be planned for us after the evening service....arriving back to our rooms around 11:00. The morning and afternoon meetings were for ministry/teaching to pastors and workers. The evening ministry was specifically directed toward the professionals and business people of the churches. Different members of the hosting church took turns providing our meals and we were certainly treated graciously. We were guest in some of the finest restaurants and homes in Zamboanga! One evening we were treated to dinner at the Officer's Club on the Philippine Air Force Base.

After leaving Zamboanga, our next stop was Davao City where we were hosted by Pastors Bert and Tess Diao. This is our third year to come here and we appreciate the consideration of this pastor and the church. The same schedule followed....morning, afternoon and evening. Leon and Bob alternated teaching. I remember Brother Bob instructing about the purpose of seminars is not ONLY to hear teaching/preaching, to be blessed and have fellowship but to hear, apply it, obey, overcome problems, and be refreshed spiritually in order to get the job done...we are talking about THE HARVEST! As Leon ministered "The set time has come", this seem to become the theme of ministry at this place. Ministry and receptivity was good in Davao.

We arrived in Cagyan D'Ore the 28th at 3:35 and were met by Pastors Bea and Emma and Pastor Emma two daughters, Flor and Rachel. We then made the two hour drive to Illigan City where the students of the Bible School had our dinner waiting. Chicken and salad! It tasted good! The weather has been hotter than usual at this time of the year and Illigan City was no exception. We spent the evening visiting, took our cold, bucket baths (you have really learn to enjoy them by now) and retired for the night with 2 fans turned on us.

Leon and I were at Harvest Time Temple with Pastors Bea and Emma for the morning service and Bob and Jeanne went to Living Word. In the evening, Leon and I went to Inner Faith with Pastors Ricky and Jean .

James joined with us for our time here in Illigan City. It was good to see him and hear him share of his ministry in the mountains here and Davao City. We had only evening seminars with the exception of one afternoon which was directed toward relationships and marriage. Leon and I shared this afternoon together. After four days in Illigan, we left on Thursday to return to Manila.

We spent a few days in Manila before leaving for Kula Lumpur, Malaysia. We were hosted by Pastors Moses and Ann Tan. They have two daughters, Michell and Rachel.

We arrived in Kula Lumpur Tuesday at 11:30. Pastor Andrew was with Pastor Moses. We went to The Tan's home and had refreshments and visited. Leon went with Pastor Moses and Ann to a prayer meeting. I stayed home. The next day Sister Ann and I prepared for a lady's meeting in the afternoon, a group of young wives/mothers in the lovely home of Sister Pauline. I was scheduled as the speaker. This was a good time. They were precious and easy to visit with. I loved them right away! I met a nice lady, Esther Lim, she offered to E-mail Carla for me! It is always good to hear from home when so far away!

Kula Lumpur is a very large and modern city. I had a feeling of being in the southern part of USA with the palm trees, etc. Kula Lumpur has twin towers taller than the Chicago Tower in Chicago. The lights of Kula Lumpur were fantastic. Most of the Christians here are either Chinese or Indian. The Malaise are born Moslems and are subject to much adversity if they publicly become Christians. You have choices of many different kinds of foods. I like it all! The Indian and Malaise foods are more hot-spicy than the Chinese. I also learned a trunk of the car is referred to as the "boot"....and grades in school are called "standards". The people are very friendly. I really enjoyed them.

We met several pastors for lunch and a time of getting acquainted. There seems to be many churches and pastors who are independent and are interested in the Full Gospel Fellowship's affiliation. Leon was scheduled to speak at a Full Gospel Businessmen's luncheon. I felt this was a good time, considering the financial difficulty in Asia at this time, I feel the men and women were encouraged and blessed by the ministry. We had evening meetings here. Pastor Moses' church is named Cross Power Tabernacle and he has three services on Sunday, two in the morning and one in the afternoon. Leon missed Bob! He ministered all three. He wanted me to take one of them, but I told him someone would get cheated! His voice made it and the last one was as exciting as the first! Of course, Leon spoke a different topic for each service. He seldom repeats himself. The first service, Leon spoke about the Holy Spirit (The Voice of a Conqueror) and after the service, a man came up and said to Leon, I don't think I have this Helper, the Holy Spirit, how may I receive this? He was a retired Chinese business man and had been attending Cross Power for only a short time. He and his wife invited us along with the Tan family for dinner. They took us to the Country Club for an excellent meal. They had to bring me utensils. I just couldn't get the "hang" of chop sticks! Theresa even peeled her prawns using her chop sticks! Amazing! I really tried! I just couldn't do it!

We had a busy, rewarding time in Kula Lumpur, Malaysia and we have yet to see exactly what plans God has for us and the Full Gospel Fellowship here.

We had one day in Manila before leaving for home. James met us at the airport for the long flight over the ocean! It had been a long, tiring, rewarding thirty-four days. We usually get to play in the warm ocean water at least once, but this time, the only time I saw the beach was when we were flying over it! Oh well! The Lord has ways to remind me "this ain't no playground, it's a battlefield"!

I Remember.....Ghana, West Africa.

We arrived about 10:00 in the evening after a 24 hour flight. We were met at the airport by Sister Almaz from Ethiopia and Pastors Solomon, Foster, Justice and Jerry from Ghana. We were very tired. They took us to our hotel, brought us food which had been prepared by Pastor Solomon's wife, Veronica. We visited until about 12:00 and retired for a short rest.

We were ready to leave by 6:30 next morning for a village, Odomasie, approximately 2 hours away. When we arrived the meeting was in progress. We were introduced and taken to our rooms to rest until the evening service. We have never seen people worship and praise like they did in Odomasie! They danced until the air was thick with dust, waving hankies, celebrating Jesus! They worship with no inhibitions. Leon explains that the word "Hallelujah" comes from two words, Hallal-jah, hallal meaning to celebrate, being clamorously foolish, rejoicing, dancing....and "Jah" is a Hebrew name for God. I believed we experienced this in Odomosie!! The Ghanians have rhythm in every inch of their bodies and they magnify the Lord with their body, soul (emotions) and spirit. I think we got a glimpse of David when he danced as the Ark of Covenant was being brought back into Jerusalem!

Sister Almaz and Leon shared the ministry time and God moved in the word of knowledge, teaching, preaching and prayer time.

Pastor Justice shared with me that he was not very impressed when he first met us at the airport, thinking "What can these two old people do?" However, after hearing Leon the first time, he kept saying, "Wow! So powerful!" The Odomasie pastors said, "You must stay with us longer, we need this teaching."

Most of the pastors are young men in their 30's. We met three pastors who were forty and above. The pastors are bible school graduates. Intelligent young men, hard workers, prayer warriors, ambitious, and zealous for evangelism. They have young families and their wives are also dedicated and called of God and very capable of ministry.

After the first week in Odomasie, we returned to the Accra area and were in churches here for the next 2 weeks. Our first meeting was scheduled with Miracle Revival Christian Center, Pastor Bernard Adams in Medina Village, the village is predominately Moslem. Of 87,000 people, all of the Christian Churches combined in Medina would amount to around 15,000. Pastor Adams church, about 3-4 years old has a membership of 800-1000. He has a small building and has two services on Sunday morning to accommodate the people. They are looking for land to rebuild.

One of the first services there, as Pastor Adams was closing the meeting, he said, "I am so impressed with 'Mama' Tena". I was surprised, wondering what impressive thing I had done!!! He continued. "The way she supports her husband while he is preaching... and she looks at him as though it is the first time she has seen him!"(smile, smile) I became almost self conscious! I tried to explain to Pastor Adams....I said, "I love the word of God and I love good preaching/teaching and Leon is the best! He seldom repeats himself and even when he does, the anointing is fresh and I am so blessed! My husband is a preacher (one who proclaims the word of God) and a teacher (one who explains the word of God) and that combination mixed with excitement and anointing is hard to beat! God has surely given Leon an "anointed sword"!

We were also with Pastor Jacob Villars, also from Medina Village and God moved with miracles of healing. His mother testified of a healing of her back. A nurse had pain in her hand and wrist and was healed. The pastor's father has Parkinson's Disease, and we were told, his father was so happy, every day the shaking is less. One young man said God gave him a song about Ezekiel! Pastor Jacob said his church has not been the same!

In Accra, Sister Almaz and Leon had separate meetings planned throughout the two weeks. We were with Pastor Solomon, Pastor Foster and Pastor Larry Johnson in East Legon, a new church of about 300. They had 2 dialects being interpreted at the same time.

Leon ministered on Joseph, "Don't let your dream die". The people received and were so encouraged.

We were in a church in the middle of the city, International Bible Worship Center, Rev Sam Ankra, pastor. This work is only 5 years old and has a membership of 3000. They have 3 services on Sunday AM. Leon ministered the first two and Sister Almaz ministered the last one (she had been with Pastor Adams for his two meetings). What a time we had! Celebrating, praise, worship as only African worshipers can do! They know how to worship to the beat of the African drums! One sister told me that I needed to just "let myself go"!

On the "other side" of Accra, we were with a young pastor, Ebow Simpson for two nights. He is 30 years old and has a degree in agricultural science, called to preach the word and pastor. His work is less than 2 years old and he has around 200 in attendance.

On Tuesday and Wednesday we went back to Rev. Ankra's IBWC for teaching. Pastor Ankra was away, in Europe, one of his assistants, Pastor Joseph welcomed us at this time. Leon taught the mid week Bible study on Tuesday and on Wednesday, he spoke to the leadership of the church. Pastor Joseph asked Leon for his notes to copy. He said for the next four weeks, he was going over this teaching line by line! Leon also left with him his outlines on the book of Ephesians.

Before going to Ghana, Leon pulled some information from the Internet about Ghana and we learned that 48% of Ghana is 15 years of age and younger, so I had an idea to take something that I might share with the children, if the opportunity availed itself. I ended up doing some workshops for Sunday school teachers, using my material. I talked to the teachers from II Peter 1:4, "we are to become partakers of His divine nature by PRACTICE". How our natures are changed by practicing God's word, by being "doers, not listeners, only". Habits are formed by doing the same thing over and over again. Jesus said "If you love me, keep my commandments". He did not say we would always "feel like" it, but as we bypass our feelings and as an act of obedience to the word of God, practice the word of God, we can become "partakers of His nature"!

Now think about not having to change our nature, but working with children, we have the privilege of helping them develop the nature of God in their young lives. As they mature into Adults, the Spirit of God develops right along with them! They can grow into strong mature Christians and whatever profession they choose in life, God will be their source! We do not know the plan God has for our children, but he does have a plan, not someday, but today! Moses' mother did not know that the destiny of a nation was in the bosom of the baby as she placed him in the basket and allowed him to float down the Nile River....but God had a plan...and he has a plan for our children today. Sunday School should be more than entertainment, keeping them quiet so as not to disturb the adults. We need to be helping them to PRACTICE the word of God! It's more than telling the stories of the Bible! They can walk in obedience today while children...and they are special in God's plan! The teachers seemed to be encouraged. I left my material for them to use. .

Sister Almaz returned to Ethiopia after three weeks and our last week there, we went to the North of Accra, Kpando. We were there for three days. Pastor Hini works in the more difficult area of Ghana, the northern part where there is still much voodoo worship and witch craft. He has established around 45 churches and has schools for disciplining workers. We were very impressed with the work of "Narrow Gate Ministries". The worship was great and so was ministry!

By the time we left Ghana, Leon was being introduced as, "a general" in God's army and "a walking bible". We have been invited back with request to stay longer.

We love the Ghana people! They made us Ghana clothes. They are warm, caring people and they have a really great sense of humor! They are enjoyable to be with.

Ghana is a peaceful place and Leon feels that Ghana is destined to be a "sending" nation for the gospel to other places in Africa. Africa needs the gospel of Christ. He loves the African people. In Africa we were in local churches! God is just as interested in the local churches in Africa as He is in the USA and in His eyes there are no international barriers....it is all His church and His body.

We feel privileged that God chose to allow us to be introduced to the Church in Ghana, West Africa!

On the way to the airport for our return trip home, one of the young pastors, Justine, said to us, "Mama and Papa, you are true missionaries. You came to us and did not spend your time in the hotel, you stayed in our homes, slept in our beds and ate our food. You touched our lives. We are so blessed." We feel that we are the ones who are blessed. They are precious people!

I Remember........Kenneth Ballard

We had been called back to our home town of Harrisburg to pastor the church. During the first year of that time, a couple of evangelist had come through town and spent the night with us. As they were preparing to leave the next morning, they prayed for us and told us that a miracle was going to take place in our church on the following Sunday. Needless to say we anticipated as to what type of miracle this was going to be......one thinks of healing, signs, wonders, etc.....we went to church with expectancy!

We had an ordinary service and at the close of the service, Leon gave a call for salvation. My cousin, Ken, left his seat and walked to the front to accept Jesus as the Lord of his life. Ken at the age of around 25 was considered our "town drunk". This was truly a miracle. God's plan for salvation, the way that God can come and live inside a person and change him, rearrange him and route him for success is absolutely the greatest miracle in the world. I have seen miracles of healing, but the way that God can change a person still amazes me!

Ken had a lot of problems at the mill where he worked, no one took him serious at first nor did they believe it would last. The men would try to lure him into going for a drink and when that didn't work they would torment him, tease him and tell him he was not a Christian. Ken came to our house one evening, feeling so remorseful...he was "laying core" in the plywood mill and the "sheet turners" would purposefully scrape his head with the sheet and say "You are not a Christian, Ken". Ken took it all he could and turned around....."You dirty blankety-blank-blank......I am a Christian, too!"

One evening we were returning from a fellowship meeting, Ken was riding in the front seat with Leon and Ken just lifted his hands and began to praise God, then he laughed and made this statement.

"Who would have ever thought that Ken Ballard would be going to heaven?!"

I saw Ken a few weeks ago and he reminded me that he had been saved for 30 years!

Ken married a great person named Dianna. They have two daughters, plus a daughter from a previous marriage. God gave Ken a gift of writing poems and songs. He has written hundreds! They are great songs and Ken sings them, too. Love it!

Ken and his family have been a blessing to us!

THE DRUNK CALLED KEN

THERE WAS A DRUNK CALLED KEN WHO WALLOWED IN THE FILTH OF SIN
FROM MORN 'TIL NIGHT THERE WAS NOTHING RIGHT HIS LIFE WAS DARK WITHIN
THEN ONE DAY IN A WONDERFUL WAY GOD'S VOICE SPOKE SOFTLY TO HIM
HE SAID IT'S ENOUGH LAY DOWN THAT STUFF AND NEVER PICK IT UP AGAIN

HIS LIFE AS CHANGED IN A MOMENT OF TIME FROM A PATH OF SIN AND SHAME
THE LOVE OF GOD FLOWED THRU HIS SOUL 'TWAS THE FLOW OF THE LATTER RAIN
HE FOUND FREEDOM FROM THE STING THAT HAD VEXED HIS TROUBLED SOUL
AND ENTERED ONTO A PATH WITH HEAVEN AS ITS GOAL
BOOZE LIKE WINE, BEER AND RUM ARE FOREVER A THING OF THE PAST
HIS SOUL HAD FOUND THE LOVE OF GOD HIS SINS WERE FOREVER CAST
INTO THE SEA OF FORGETFULNESS COMPLETELY OUT OF HIS SIGHT
NO MORE BARS AND CLUBS FOR KEN BECAUSE GOD MADE ALL THINGS RIGHT

THE WINDS MAY BLOW AND THE STORMS SWEEP BUT
NOTHING CAN SHAKE WITHIN
THE GOD GIVEN HOPE IN THE HEART OF HIM WHO WAS
THE DRUNK CALLED KEN
THE LOVE OF GOD SO FLOODS HIS SOUL THAT NOTHING
COULD EVER ERASE
NO PLEASURE THIS OLD WORLD COULD GIVE WILL EVER
TAKE GOD'S PLACE

POEM WRITTEN FOR KEN BALLARD BY E.W. ANGLIN 11-30-
69

(Ken has two cassette/cd recordings of songs that he has composed. He
and his family would be a blessing to be invited to your church. He and
his wife have beautiful testimonies plus he and his daughters would bless
you with their music.)

I Remember.....Vera, my Mother

The month of May is the time set aside for us to remember our Mothers and to pay tribute to them, and so, I would like to take advantage of this time and share with you my mother.

I am very blessed that I still have the joy of having my mother alive and well! She is 87 years of age. She still lives alone, takes care of her needs, drives her car and has a full social life with many friends and family near her.

I love going to Mother's house for a visit. She can still cook up the best pot of beans, served with southern fried potatoes and corn bread....in the world. Mother has a great sense of humor and enjoys people!

Mother was saved in 1934 and she told me that she was seven months pregnant with me when she was baptized in water by my uncle, Rev. E.W. Anglin. So Mother has served the Lord faithfully for these "60 - something" years. She has seldom (if ever) gone a full week without meeting together with the Church to worship and learn of Jesus. Mother has been a faithful member of the church in Harrisburg, Oregon over the 48 years that she has lived in Oregon.

"Faithfulness" is a fruit of the Spirit that has certainly been cultivated in her life and I am thankful for that heritage. Another attribute is her tremendous love and trust in her savior, Jesus. She has believed Him for healing for her family and each of us (her children) have been recipients of miracles because of her prayers.

My brother, Roy, had a ruptured appendix when he was about five years of age. The doctor did not want to operate because it was too late. The nurse insisted, the doctor did not believe he would live. He was healed through the power of prayer!

I was born during the depression time. My mother did not have enough to eat to produce milk for me. I was put on a bottle and was allergic to cow's milk. Mother told me when I was five months old, I weighed nine pounds with all my blankets around me. Someone suggested goat's milk…and goat's milk was expensive. Someone gave mother a nanny goat so I could have milk.

My younger brother, Perry experienced an accident and cut the main artery in his hand. He was a "free bleeder" and the hand would not heal. Perry was about four years of age. Every time the doctors would change his bandage, (weekly) he would start bleeding and they would have to give him blood transfusions. I remember Mother fasted and prayed for over one week. She went five days without drinking water. When the time came for another bandage change, his hand was healed!

When my little sister, Doneta was about 5 years old, she was accidentally shot. The bullet went in just below her temple bone, traveled through her throat, punctured her voice box and missed all the other vital organs and lodged in her shoulder. She came home well and healed! Mother knows by experience the power of prayer!

Mother has been a volunteer help in the office of the Full Gospel Fellowship for years and has faithfully helped with the monthly mailing of our newsletters. Daily, I give thanks to the Lord for the health and life of my mother. This is truly a blessing from God.

Vera, my Mother – Part Two

The month of May has been set aside to remember Mothers.....
and today I am remembering MY MOTHER, Vera Anglin. Mother
went home to be with Jesus on January 30th. We learned over the
Christmas holidays that the cancer had spread to Mother's liver. I
cannot tell you what an ache was in our hearts when the doctors told
us she had from 4-6 weeks. I could not bear to think of her dying a
horrible, painful death. I wanted her to have good days until He took
her home....and she did. They gave her a pain patch. She was not sick
to her stomach, nor did she experience pain. She was alert until the
last day and just "went to sleep."

The last night before she went into the "coma", the family was in
her room and we sat around and sang some of the old hymns that she
loved. It was a very precious time. I was not ready to give her up. I
said that to my son, Ric, and he just looked at me and said, "I know,
Mom, but you know what? Grandmother is ready." Mother had
asked the hospice nurse how she could just go to sleep and not wake
up and that is just what she did. I don't think there is any way that
you can prepare yourself for the finality of giving up your mother.
Others who have been here tell me that you never stop missing them!
I just wonder, how long do you cry??? I have missed her every day! I
am sure that I will miss her for the rest of my life. In twenty-eight
days, Mother would have celebrated her 89th birthday.

Mother left us examples of faith and faithfulness that has and
will impact our lives forever. She had served our Lord for 64 years
and loved her church families, the first one was the Assembly of Jesus
Christ in Mangum, Oklahoma. She then moved to Harrisburg,
Oregon and was faithful and active in Valley Christian Center for 51
years. Mother knew how to pray and receive her petitions from God.
As my younger brother was saying his good-by to Mother on his last
visit home, he told her, "Mom, I am scared to death to live without
your prayers." However, we know that her prayers will live on!

Mother is singing the "song of the redeemed" we talked about heaven a lot the last couple of weeks. We read about heaven. She was anxious to see her mother and her brother, George, who raised her... and of course Daddy. Mother passed on with amazing grace and dignity. My esteem for her mounted as I watched her face death. There was no fear...surely all "sting" had been removed as she passed from this life to the next possessing the same faith by which she had lived.

Tears still come without warning. Mother was my friend. She was a good mother and she gave us her best. As I said, I am sure I will miss her forever!

I would like to say here how that I have loved and appreciated Leon's parents, Archie and Luella Willis. They welcomed me into the family and treated me with love. I enjoyed them! They treated me like a daughter!

Luella was so gifted with writings and expressing herself with poems. I want to share one with you!

THINGS YOU CAN'T BUY....by Luella Willis (Leon' mother)

I was wishing that I had the money to buy,
All my dreams as I sat by the fire.
What a life I would live; what riches I would give,
What more could a heart desire.
When my sweet little mother said softly to me,
"There are some things, my child, you can't buy,
You can't buy love; it comes down from above,
Or a moment of time when you die."
"You can't buy the summer in wintertime;
You can't buy the spring in the fall.
And no matter my child, how much wealth you have,
Not one day can you recall.
You can't buy back you good name;
One time you have blacked it with sin,
Only Jesus' blood can cleanse your heart,
And make it white again."
"You can't buy the sunshine at twilight;
You can't buy the moonlight at dawn.

You can't buy your youth when you are growing old,
Or your life when the heartbeat is gone.
You can't buy you way into heaven,
Though wealth may hold power untold.
And when you lose your mother, you can't buy another,
If you owned all the world and its gold."

I Remember......Rachel Gordon

Rachel and her husband, Preston, moved to my small town of Harrisburg in 1974. They moved from the busy, crowded San Diego, California area and purchased a small western clothing business. The business had a "side" facility with printing equipment. My Husband, Leon and I were pastors of a church in this town and Leon used the printing equipment for our needs at the church.

We would go out for pizza, snacks, and got acquainted with Preston and Rachel. They would ask us questions about religion and our church.....Preston started with "what are your thoughts on evolution, or how do you feel about the Darwin theory". Rachel had been raised in the Catholic Schools but was not a "practicing Catholic".

One day I went into their store and Rachel walked up to me and said, "Tena, I believe in Jesus, now, what do I do?" I asked her if she could get away from the store, we walked down to the river (about two blocks away) and we talked about Jesus and His plan of salvation, the difference in religion and a relationship, and I prayed with Rachel. She invited the Lord into her heart and received Him as her Savior.

One day Leon was in the shop to buy himself a pair of boots. When he started to pay for his boots, Preston said "no"...they were a gift. Leon insisted to pay and said if he was not allowed to pay then he would put them back on the shelf. (Leon felt they were struggling in the business and wanted to help.) Preston said, "Leon, I will make a deal with you, if you will take the boots as a gift, I will come to church on Sunday." What else could Leon do? Well, they came to church. Preston made a commitment to the Lord, too and they were baptized.

Rachel became a very close friend. I don't know if you are aware of the fact that a preacher-pastor's wife is not an easy life. Much is expected of this person. However, a pastor's wife is a normal woman

183

and needs a friend that she can trust and does not judge her for her short comings and failures. Rachel was that friend to me. If I was discouraged, upset, experiencing feelings hard to overcome, Rachel was there. She never seemed to judge me badly....helped me to get my feelings going in the right direction and overcome my obstacle at that time. I really feel that Rachel was a God-send to me at the right time. She let me "vent" or "rejoice". Rachel was not a "yes" person. She always "said it like it is".....when I was wrong, she told me. I really loved Rachel. I do not understand why the Lord chose to take her "home" at this time, but we can trust him and his timing. Rachel was turning 66 on the birthday of February 27 and was going to retire from her position at her job after about 28 years.

Rachel had been treated for about a month for sinus problems because she had a headache and difficulty breathing. She called me on Christmas eve...and the doctor after some test, had told her that she has a deterioration of her skull-bone and it is probably malignant. Our grandson was here for Christmas and I rode back to Harrisburg with them to Rachel's house. We went to the hospital on the next day. They found that the entire left side of her lungs were completely filled with tumors and a large tumor was covering the breath-way at the top of her lungs. It was not operable. Rachel's brother and family came to be with her and she went home to be with the Lord on January 5th.

I still miss Rachel and I am thankful she was in my life as a friend-a gift from God!

I Remember.....Lee and Linda Drogensen

I remember Lee and Linda..... We first met them on a Sunday in the early '70's. After church, Leon, Ken Ballard and I went out to the Round Table to eat. Linda must have overheard our conversation; they were leaving the restaurant at the same time that we were leaving. Leon was paying for our meal and Ken and I went on ahead. Linda stopped us and asked us to pray with her. She said she use to go to church but not anymore. She said her husband drinks and she drinks with him. I introduced her to Ken and told her that Ken use to drink, but God saved him and delivered him from the alcohol and now he works with a group of teenagers called the Lively Stones who evangelize and sing. Ken said, "We are singing at the church this afternoon, come and join us."

By this time, Lee had also come out of the restaurant, gotten into his car and was "on the horn" for Linda to "let's go". Linda asked me to go over and meet Lee. Lee was somewhat intoxicated, got out of the car, came around to Linda's side, opened the door and HELPED her into the car. As they were driving away, Linda said to me, "I live at 265 West Third Street in Junction City, come and get me and take me to church!"

Wow! I thought, "What if that man gives me a whoopin' when I get there". I didn't know what to expect. I left Leon and Ken at the church and found 265 West Third Street and walked up to the door. Linda met me with her arms around a LARGE family bible. She was ready to go to church! I asked her about Lee and she said he was passed out on the bed. When we arrived at the church, I followed Linda right up to the front row. Ken and The Lively Stones began to sing and worship. Linda didn't like the new songs and asked if they knew some of the old gospel songs like "I'll Fly Away". Linda enjoyed the service, God touched her and she was blessed. One of the young men, Jeff, prayed for Linda that God would deliver her from the alcohol that was still in her body. Linda and I had a good visit when I took her home and I promised to call her.

The next day was Memorial Day, I tried to call, but no answer. I called again on Wednesday. She was happy to hear from me and even recognized my voice. Linda told me that Lee said, "My mama was a Lutheran, Her mama was a Lutheran and I am a Lutheran and I will be a Lutheran until I die! I said, "Linda, if Lee will go with you to the Lutheran church, you go with him". She said she would.

It was a pleasant surprised the next Sunday when Lee and Linda came to church! They went to the early service at the Lutheran Church and then Linda asked him to go with her to "her church". We had a great service. We worshiped and Leon ministered the Word. Linda said that Lee didn't say a word when they got in the car and about half way to Junction City he said ,"Linda, when I die, I want that man to preach my funeral". Lee had felt the presence of the Lord. He went home, gathered up all his empty beer bottles, poured out the full ones, and gave them to a neighbor-hood "kid" to take in for return deposit.

Lee never missed another meeting. I cannot tell you what a blessing Lee and Linda were to our church body! Lee came by the church every day on his way home from work. Leon was doing a lot of remodeling and there was always lots of work to do to maintain the old building. Lee would help Leon in any way that he was needed! Anytime there was a bazaar, baked food sale, or cleaning the church, you could count on Linda! She was a worker! They began a ministry of visitation to the Nursing Home. This was a needy area and the people really loved them and looked forward to the visits. They were faithful! Faithfulness has a high priority in God's eyes! Faithfulness is a fruit of the Spirit.(Galatians 5:22) However, faithfulness was not the only fruit that we observed manifested in their lives as they served God. They loved the Lord and loved our church body. Linda became a very close friend of my mother. They were "buddies" for years! Lee passed away a few months before Mother. Lee and Mother have surely heard the Master say to them, "Well done my good and faithful servants, you have been faithful over a few things, I will put you in charge of many things, enter into the joy of your Lord." Matthew 25:22 Linda moved to Florida to be with her family. We will always love and remember LEE AND LINDA DROGENSEN!

I Remember.......Val Chambers

I was reading where Paul writing to the Ephesians said, "I make mention of you in my prayers". Over the years, I have appreciated that because much of the time, we feel that the only prayers that God hears are the ones that we spend on our knees in agony and travail. I know there are times for "on the knee prayers and travail", but today I am remembering my friend, Val.

Our families became acquainted through our husbands working together at a plywood mill. We developed a friendship and enjoyed swimming, fishing, gold panning in the Trinity River of northern California. We also liked to ride motorcycles and go on hunting trips.

Val did not believe in God. When the subject would come up, she would say, "don't talk to me about that stuff because I do not want to hear it". Even after leaving northern California, we kept in touch with each other, sometimes not hearing from each other for months, but still in touch. Sometimes, she would call me when one of her children was sick and ask me to pray for them. Once, I asked her why she did this since she didn't believe in God and she would just laugh and say, "Well, just in case it works!" I really loved Val, she was a very precious friend.

One day, Val called to tell me that she had cancer. I went to the hospital with her the day of her mastectomy. Val and I talked. I would say, "Val, let me tell you about Jesus and explain to you His plan for you to be saved". Val would say, "OK, but not now"....she kept putting me off. We were in Pizza Hut (next door to her business) and I told her again that I wanted to talk to her about Jesus. She would look around and say "Not here". I said "when, Val?".....I talked about Jesus as much as I could.

Many times during the day, I would mention Val's name to the Lord. I didn't even know how to pray for her. I would feel so frustrated. This is basically the way I would pray: Lord, please draw

Val to you. Please give her a desire to know you. Prepare Val for salvation. Jesus, somehow reveal Yourself to Val. I can't stand to think of Val going out of this life and not knowing you. I just prayed along those lines on a daily basis.

Leon and I were in Montana visiting our daughter and family when we received a call. Dick had made the call for Val and Val was crying. She said, "He was here for three days and then I woke up and he is gone, I have looked everywhere for Him, but He is not here". I said, "Who, Val?" She said "Jesus! He was here but now he is gone". I cannot tell you the excitement in my heart!

I told her that Jesus must love her so much to reveal himself to her in this way. I asked her if she would like to pray and received Him as her Savior. She said yes, that she wanted to do this. I asked her if she believed in Him. She said that she had talked to Him for three days. Of course she believed in Him. Val prayed, confessing her faith in Jesus and asking Him to be her Savior! Our God is so faithful!

Leon and I went on to Idaho to be with Pastors Ron and Joann Beeman when Dick called again saying that Val was going to the hospital and it looked pretty bad. Leon put me on a plane and I flew to Eugene and spent a couple of days with Val before she passed away. We talked about Jesus. I told her that I had believed in Him all of my life and yet, I have never had the privilege of seeing Him as she had. He answered my prayers! He drew Val to Him. He gave her faith! How much He loves !

I Remember.....My daughter, Carla

When my daughter, Carla, was 15 years of age, she did not like me very much. I would not let her go to parties with her friends from school. Drugs had been introduced into our small town. She told me that I was ruining her life and that I could not choose her friends for her. She said she did not want to drink or do drugs, she just wanted to be with her friends.

I told her that I could just give over and let her do this and then she would like me, but that would be just like "handing her over to Satan" and when she got all messed up, take her back and help her the best that I could, but I said to her, "Carla, I just love you too much, I just cannot do this!"

On her 16th birthday, we were in church and I saw Carla go back to the nursery. I followed her to talk with her. I asked her to give herself the best 16th birthday present she could ever receive. Just give yourself to Jesus and let Him be the Lord of your life. She said that she could not do this because her friends were not Christians and she could not be one by herself. I told her this was a lie that the devil had put in her mind. Her friends are going to need someone who is strong to help them in their lives....and "Carla, you can be that person.",

At the end of the service, she walked up to the front and made that commitment to the Lord. She has not looked back. She did become that strong person that her friends needed. I am so proud of the person that Carla is! At one time, at a women's renewal meeting, the minister, Sharon Miller, called her up for ministry and said to her, "Carla, you have been raised as a delicate plant, loved, cherished, protected. When people look at you, they consider you as delicate. But you are not delicate in your spirit, you are a WAR HORSE, fierce in battle with a determined spirit, not relenting or giving any ground to the devil. You persevere with the strength of a WAR HORSE that has been trained and disciplined for battle."

A couple years ago, Carla was diagnosed with breast cancer, both breasts, and underwent a double mastectomy. Her faith and attitude was amazing! We cried together, each of us not understanding why. She was told by the doctors that the cancer was hormonally caused. She had earlier had a hysterectomy, however her ovaries had been left. Leon and I were in the Philippine Islands and I spoke with her. They wanted to remove her ovaries. She said to me, "They are taking the last of my female parts." I said, "Carla, the Bible says that as a woman thinks in her heart, so is she, so as long as you have a mind and can think and you have a heart (will and emotions) you are a woman!" Praise the Lord!

Well, her love relationship with the Lord brought her through all of this! She is strong and is an amazing woman!

Carla has exercised rule over her own spirit. I give thanks to the Lord for this. She is a "WAR HORSE" She continues to stands against the enemy!

Carla is still looking at battles in her own world, but her faith is strong and she continues to battle with the faith that through the Holy Spirit, she will be the winner.

At this time, Carla has a responsible position as Medical Records manager in a large retirement facility and she is taking classes (college courses) to get her degree in this field. She is amazing!

Carla has a son, Michael and a daughter, Lindsay. Michael is married to Shannon and they have three children. Twins, Braedon and Grace (Age 9) and Bria (age 4) . Carla is pretty proud!
Leon and I are pretty proud, also! Love those great-grandkids! Lindsay is not married....yet.

Carla is married to Mark Guyett. Mark has a great voice and has a music ministry. Carla has learned sign language and she "signs" and dances as Mark sings. Leon and I love to listen and watch!

Carla has influenced people in her world and has strong friends because of her strong faith and love for Jesus. Leon and I have been so thankful and know we are blessed to have Carla for our daughter!

I LOVE YOU, JESUS, AND THANK YOU FOR MY FAMILY!

I Remember....My son Ric

I am remembering to thank Jesus for his great love and mercy to our family!

When our son, Ric, was 6 years of age, he was diagnosed with "brights disease". This is a disease of the kidneys due to a sreptococcus infection. The kidneys were deteriorating and he was constantly losing red blood cells and albumin (protein) through the kidneys. His kidney specialist kept him in controlled activity. No play ground activities, no bike riding. Leon taught him to play chess, would carry him down to the lake. His activities were so limited. When he was in the 4th grade, she said that she had been to a special teaching about this disease. Children who were confined, like Ric, were no better off and the ones who had been allowed to live normal lives were not worse, so she wanted to release Ric to normal activities. Ric begin to train for track and did great! It was fun to see him involved in sports! He then went out for wrestling! He excelled in this sport! We were so proud of him! When he was sixteen, his doctor requested a kidney biopsy to determine if both kidneys were damaged or only one. The report: both kidneys. They told us that eventually Rick would need a kidney transplant, probably by the time he would be thirty....perhaps, by that time a kidney transplant will have become more perfected. Otherwise he would have to go on kidney dialysis. The future was somewhat shaky.

Ric has always been a "believer" however, we were in a camp meeting at Wallowa Lake. During a youth meeting, he walked up to the front and took the microphone from Marty and made a statement, "I am not a Christian, but I want to be one, I have an ache in my gut that I want to get rid of." He made his stand and commitment!

When Ric was twenty, he was working on a ranch in Eastern Oregon. He called home that he had gotten very sick and had gone to the doctor. The doctor was quite alarmed, told him he should not be on a horse or tractor either one and wanted to put him in the Portland hospital at once. We asked Ric to come home and see his kidney specialist and we would follow her recommendation.

Sunday morning at church, Leon was asking the church to pray for Ric. We were so afraid that his kidneys were deteriorating faster than they had thought. A woman in our church, Marge Olander, stood and said that she felt if our church as a body will fast and pray for Rick on Monday, God would heal him. I understand that even some children and men missed meals and prayed for Ric. He came home on Tuesday and went to see his doctor on Wednesday! She told him that he had never been so good! "This," she said, "was the best test he had ever had!" There were a few red blood cells and a little albumin.....but he had never tested so good!

Ric has never had any more trouble with his kidneys! God did a miracle! If you know anything about this disease....you don't get well without a miracle! God is so awesome! Rick is fifty-five today and the picture of health! Ric married a wonderful girl! Vickie is her name and she is so loved by Ric's family!

Now we have another miracle to report!

Ric likes to exercise, belongs to a gym. and "works our" faithfully. A few years ago he bought himself a bicycle. They live about 30 miles from their work and the road to home is all up hill. During the summer months, Ric rides his bike home! He has talked about riding his bike from his house to our house....200 miles....5 mountain passes....and he wants to do this in two days. They were at our house to celebrate Leon's birthday the end of June and Ric said, "Mom, I think I may have to quit riding my bike." I asked why and he said when he hurt his knee while wrestling (in High School)...it just keeps acting up and riding the bike seems to irritate it more.

Ric and Vickie went to church with us the next morning and we had a visiting minister. We had never met him. As he played his guitar and began to praise and worship, he stopped and said, "God is healing someone's knee...right now!" WOW! This was soooo good! Ric accepted this gift of healing from God!

Now, our "Son by love", Mark, also enjoys riding the bike and they made plans! On October 6th, Ric left his house at 7:30 am and Mark left our house. Their plans were to meet in Mitchell. This was ALMOST half way. Ric rode 110 miles, three mountain passes and two flat tires, didn't quite make it to Mitchell. We took them back to where Ric left off the next morning. (Leon, Vickie, Carla and I all met them for a rendezvous at the small town of Mitchell on Friday evening. We ate dinner together spent the night, talked about the day, etc.(- love being with my kids!)

Ric and Mark rode to the top of the Ochoco Pass, going up another long mountain pass. Rick said his legs started cramping up and just quit working. He thinks he over loaded his muscles the first day! But.......the old knee he says is still pumping! They are already making plans for next year!

I am so thankful for the faithfulness of God, for His mercies and His love!

Vickie, was diagnosed with breast cancer in 1998 and she is also receiving good reports of healing. God is so good to us. Vickie has been such a great blessing in our family.

She is a wonderful person...and after 34 years of marriage, still treats my son like a king! This makes a "mother's heart" so appreciative.

Here is another testimony! About 2007, Ric was having lots of pain in the kidney area and went to the doctor. They did lots of test and determined that the urethra (the little tube connection from the kidney to the bladder} was "kinked". They put him in the hospital to insert a tube thing to hold it and keep it from kinking.

I asked Ric if the doctors said anything about the damage that had been done to his kidneys during the "bright disease" years. He said, "They do not believe that I ever had that disease." When he mentioned that according to biopsy reports, both were deteriorating. They said "you had biopsies? " He said that he had, and they could not explain it. His kidneys did not show any signs of that problem! He had received total healing!

Ric has always been a "believer" however, in the last few years he has stepped into a ministry of teaching.. He said he ran from the call and gift of teaching but made a decision to surrender to it and he is doing great at teaching. He teaches in his local church and during travels with us.

I am so thankful and so proud of Ric and Vickie!
Thank you, Jesus! I LOVE YOU!

I Remember....Hell

Having been raised in the Church, some of my earliest and most vivid memories are involved there. When I was very young, Mother would take me to revival meetings. Fiery Evangelist would come for two, sometimes three weeks meetings-every night! Now these Evangelist each had their own very vivid descriptions of Hell, and they could preach about it until you could almost feel the fire touching your toes. At a very young age, I developed a healthy fear and respect of that place and decided that was one place that I did not plan to visit.

It has been many years since I have heard about HELL from the pulpit. It is a real place. Hell is a place prepared by God the same way that HEAVEN is prepared by God. At the close of this age, we have two choices. We will either hear Jesus say, "Come, you blessed of my Father, inherit the kingdom prepared for you from the foundations of the earth." or we will hear Him say, "Depart from Me, accursed ones, into the eternal fire which has been prepared for the devil and his angels."[Matthew 25:34,41] Eternal punishment or Eternal life.

It is alarming to me that today's generation is not so concerned about the righteousness of God and living according to the teachings of the bible. Situation ethics has replaced the absolutes of a Holy God. Lying is a normal reaction among our youth today, even among our Christian young people. Immorality, impurity without guilt or true repentance is running rampant not only in the world, but in our churches. We just don't hear a lot about SIN today. God hates SIN as much today as He ever has.

Please indulge me as I refresh our memories concerning what the bible tells us about HELL.

I believe that Jesus spoke of HELL more than He spoke of HEAVEN.

Matthew 10:28 "Do not fear those who can kill the body, rather fear Him who is able to destroy both soul and body in HELL."

Matthew 13:41,42 "The Son of Man will send forth His angles, and they will gather out of His kingdom all stumbling blocks and those who commit lawlessness and will cast them into the furnace of fire; in that place there shall be weeping and gnashing of teeth."

Mark 9:43-48- This scripture lets us know that nothing is too extreme in order to keep us from going to this place!

Luke 16:23 - The story of Lazarus and the rich man, the rich man was in Hades and in agony in the flame. He wanted Lazarus to just come and dip his finger in water and touch it to his tongue.

2 Peter 2nd chapter speaks of those who are destined for this destruction. PLEASE TAKE TIME TO READ IT!

2 Peter 3:1-18 (verse 10) "But the day of the Lord will come like a thief, in which the heavens will pass away with a roar and the elements will be destroyed with intense heat, and the earth and its works will be burned up.(verse 11) Since all these things are to be destroyed in this way, what sort of people ought you to be in holy conduct and godliness, looking for and hastening the coming of the day of God, on account of which the heavens will be destroyed by burning and the elements will melt with intense heat! But according to His promise, we are looking for new heavens and a new earth, in which righteousness dwells."

Revelation 14:10-18 and 19:20 Speaks about this "lake of fire which burns with fire and brimstone".

Revelation 20:10-15 "And I saw the dead, both great and small standing before the throne and books were opened....another book was open which is the "book of life" and the dead were judged according to the things which were written in the books, according to their deeds....and if anyone's name was not found written in the book of life, they were thrown into the lake of fire."

Revelation 21:8 "But for the cowardly and unbelieving and abominable and murderers and immoral persons and sorcerers and idolaters and all liars, their part will be in the lake that burns with fire and brimstone, which is the second death."

We are saved from HELL because of the blood of the Lord Jesus Christ as we receive Him as our Savior and Redeemer. Because we accept this gift of salvation, and we make Him our Lord, He, through His Holy Spirit takes up residence within our spirits and He begins to change our desires into His desires. As we began to obey and live according to the "things which are written in the books" our nature is changed. Philippians 2:13, "For it is God who is at work in me causing me to desire to do His pleasure".

The ultimate purpose of God is not only to save us from HELL but to reveal His nature through His people and God is glorified as we are changed.

I Remember....A good Lesson Learned

It must have been about 1980 - one of our many trips to Canada. We planned a stop in Vanderhoof to spend some time with Abe & Kathy Klausen. Kathy had made some homemade rolls and chowder...I remember how good that tasted!

The next day a Bible study and baptism had been scheduled so we traveled about 30 miles on a graveled road to an Indian village. In a home, Leon preached to a room-full of people who had gathered there for ministry. I remember that it was a good time of ministry, however, the mosquitoes were in such swarms that Leon was nervous about opening his mouth and getting a mouthful of mosquitoes. We were near a lake and I'm just sure this was the breeding grounds for Canada.

After the Bible study we headed toward the lake for the baptism service. Brother Abe asked Leon if he would assist in the baptism. There were around 13 candidates. Abe baptized the 1st one.....in the name of the Father, the Son and the Holy Ghost. It was the first time I had ever witnessed anyone being baptized in this formula! Abe turned to Leon and asked that he baptize the next one, who happened to be Abe's oldest son. Leon baptized him in the name of the Lord Jesus Christ. Abe baptized the 3rd one and Leon the 4th and so on until all were baptized. This was quite the lesson for me! I thought "Well, Lord, what are you going to do with this". All were baptized in faith, believing on the Lord Jesus Christ for salvation.

The differences were never discussed between Leon and Abe.

I continue to thank God for the Full Gospel Fellowship, for His direction, a definite change in attitude, deliverance from doctrinal bondage and a leading and the freedom to receive and love all that He has received. I thank God for His great, big, wonderful family!

I thank God for Brother and Sister Welch who had the vision and courage to receive and love Leon and me.

I Remember....My Grandchildren

I always enjoyed my family, every phase and activity of Ric and Carla's world. I wanted to be involved and was so proud of them.

When Carla became a grown up adult person, she became my best friend. One time I asked Leon if guys had best friends that they talk to, you know, and he thought for a minute and said "Well, Ric....". So, we raised up our "best friends".

I didn't know that you could ever experience these feelings again, but along came our grandchildren. I remember when Michael (Carla's son) was born, I was just overwhelmed with this same love for him that had been there for Carla and Ric! A few years later, Carla gave us a little granddaughter, Lindsay! It was so fun to have a little girl added to our lives! Life is good!

They lived near us and we enjoyed these children to the fullest! They grew up in church, their grandpa (Papa Leon) was a preacher man and Michael started when he was quite young praying and preaching. Before preaching, if Michael was in the room, Leon would call him up for Michael to pray for him before he preached. I think he was about four years old and he had us all seated in our living room and he preached about David! He preached about him being in the lion's den, all the stories he could think of, David was the one! Then he wanted to pray for everyone and when he came to his little sister, Lindsay, he laid his hands on her head and asked the Lord to help her do everything that he said. (Smile)

We took Michael and Lindsay lots of places with us. We even took them about three times to Oklahoma, Missouri and Louisiana. During these trips, we stopped at most of the historical markers along the way and Leon gave history lessons. (Leon loves history). Going down the side of the Mississippi River, we stopped at many places where the battles were fought during the civil war. Michael asked about the war, were they fighting over slavery? I told him that was part of it, but some of the southern states wanted to leave the Union.

If the South would have won the war, the United States would be carved up like Europe is today into different countries. Michael said "Oh, that's why they call us the UNITED States of America!" We enjoyed the time with Michael and Lindsay. We did lots of camping trips and enjoyed being grandparents.

Now, time has passed and Michael and his wife, Shannon, have blessed us with great-grandchildren. It is hard to understand the great love that just keeps on keeping on! We were so excited when we heard that they were going to have TWINS! A little boy and a little girl came into our world, Braedon and Grace! What fun! A few years later, here came Bria! The twins are now almost ten years old and Bria is five and we have just learned that in April there will be another one....or maybe two. I do thank the Lord for his blessings and the joy that comes with a family.

Lindsay lives in Brookings, Oregon and she is not married. I want to share a poem that Leon's mom wrote for my son, Ric. He was their first grandchild. Written by: Luella Willis

My dear little grandson, in years you are only three,
But you just can't know the memories you bring back to me
Of another little lad who is your father now.
It just don't seem possible somehow,
But he looks at me with eyes as blue as your own,
I just can't realize, so many years have flown.
But I look into my mirror, and my once brown hair is gray,
And Father Time has chased the roses from my cheeks away.
And my step is not as quick, my dear little lad,
As when the little boy I held on my lap was your Dad;
But is seems my heart is more full of love than before.
Maybe it's because I've learned to appreciate a little boy more.
We live one day at a time, never more to return.
No matter how much our hearts o're happy memories may yearn;
But in you, little grandson, a great miracle I see,
For God has returned again my little boy to me.

November 24, 2010...I received a phone call from Grace. Everyone was excited. The family had been to the doctor's office and with the help of ultra sound, the family had seen the baby. Grace told me, "we are going to have a baby girl!" We were happy and excited to know this.

November 25th....Thanksgiving day. Leon and I were at Ric and Vickie's for the holiday. Carla called and was so upset. Shannon had lost the baby! Michael called his mother and she met him at the hospital.

Shannon was 4 months along, The nurses wrapped the baby in a little blanket so Carla could see her. Carla said, " I have to hold her!" Carla said, "Mom, she just fit in the palm of my hand and she was perfect! Her little legs, arms, feet, toes, hands, fingers were perfect and she was growing some hair! Michael came in and held her. They cried together!

They named her Violet.

I told Carla and Michael that I believe in heaven and I believe that Violet is alive in heaven! I can visualize My Mother and Leon's Mom assigned to the nursery of heaven! She is being loved and cared for. They will raise her up and tell her all about her family on earth and when we meet her in heaven, we will not be strangers. She will know us!

I am so thankful for that hope and faith....we will see her again and enjoy this little girl.

I remember.....my Daddy, Robert Lee Anglin

My Daddy was a hard working, responsible person. He was born on April 15, 1904. He grew up in and around Mangum, Oklahoma. During that time, if you were allowed to go to school through the 8th grade, you were considered educated. I think Daddy went through the 5th grade and then he was taken out of school to work on the farm.

He was working (farming) for Uncle Ode Epps when he and Mother were married in 1927. Mother was seventeen years of age. He also worked for Dr. Pearson. Daddy did the farming. Mother helped with house work and the farming. She and Dr. Pearson's wife, McKinley, became really good friends.

Daddy worked on the WPA (Public Works Administration). He helped with the building of the library and the armory building in Mangum. Daddy worked on the Shelter Belt, helping to plant trees and did "odd" jobs during the depression years.

Daddy learned to weld and went to work at the Air Force Base in Altus, Oklahoma. He helped to build airplanes. In 1942, we moved to Oakland, California and Daddy worked in a Shipyard. Then we moved to Del Rio, Texas (another Air Force Base) and was living there when the war ended.

We moved to Denison, Texas. Daddy and Joe Anthony went into business together under the name, "A & A Welding Shop". It did not support two families, so Daddy sold out to Joe and we headed for Oregon, via Mangum. We left for Oregon on May 20, 1946. Some of Daddy's family had moved to Oregon and reported there was plenty of work available. The family could work all summer in the fields. (picking beans, strawberries, weeding...)

Daddy went to work in a plywood mill located near Junction City in about 1950 and worked there until he retired, about 1969.

Daddy always worked hard and supported his family through all the difficult years. He went to church with us and supported the church financially. He always believed in Jesus.

We always knew he loved us. He was a quite person. He did not have a lot to say.

Daddy passed away April 20, 1986. He and Mother were married fifty-nine years. I am thankful that he was my Daddy! I loved him!

I REMEMBER...My Father By Love, Archie Willis

When I married Leon, I married into a wonderful family! His Mom and Dad accepted me into the family as a daughter! I knew I was loved.

Archie was a good man, hard working, responsible, honorable, and trustworthy.

Leon's mother was a great Christian, a godly woman and had taken her boys to church faithfully. She told me that when the boys were younger that Archie went to church with them, however, since moving to Harrisburg, he only goes to church on special occasions. He would drive Luella into town for church, then go to a local restaurant and drink coffee with friends.

The Pastor of the Church resigned and Leon was asked to accept the pastorate. We moved back to Harrisburg from Central Point and accepted this offer. It seemed we had been there for several years. Leon's Mom said one Sunday morning Archie chose to go with her to church. From that time on he went faithfully and supported the Church financially. I believe that he had made that commitment and I believe he communicated with the Lord.

One time I was riding into town with Archie and I asked him the question, "Archie, have you ever been baptized?"

He laughed and said, "Oh! I have been dunked lots of times."

I said, "Archie, you know what I mean, have you ever been baptized, because of your faith in Jesus?"

He told me, "No, he had not."

For some reason he did not choose to be baptized.

In 1978 Archie had a series of strokes and was severally handicapped. He learned to use a walker and seemed to be improving but, another stroke happened. His prognosis was not good. He could only squeeze our hands to answer "yes" or "no" to questions. The doctors were surprised that he continued to live. He lived three weeks.

We took turns staying with him 24/7. We did not want him to be alone. Archie could understand us as we talked. I think he wanted to be baptized but he could not speak to tell us himself. When different ones came to see him and talked about the Lord, Archie would cry.

One day as I was driving to the hospital for my turn, I thought, "I will ask Luella about baptizing Archie."

Well, she was tired and went home. I forgot to ask her.

When I remembered that I wanted to do that, I just decided to do it myself. So I put a towel underneath Archie's head and put some water into a cup.

I said, "Archie, I know that you know Jesus, that you believe in Him, I believe that you have repented, received Him as your personal Savior and because of this, I am going to baptize you in the name of the Lord Jesus Christ."

I poured water from a cup on Archie's head. I truly believe that I was directed by the Lord to do this. He could not speak to ask us to do this. Shortly after this was done, his breathing changed. I believe he was at peace.

I called Luella, she came back to the hospital and Archie went home to be with the Lord.

The Lord is so faithful! I know that Archie and Luella are enjoying the pleasures of heaven together. Someday, we will see them again!

I remember....I was healed of Psoriasis and Allergies

Psoriasis is a chronic skin disease characterized by reddish, scaly patches.

For a number of years I struggled to cope with this problem. I checked with a doctor and it was diagnosed as "psoriasis" and there was not cure for it. It only could be controlled with medicine applied to it. It itched continually! It was on the back of my neck and up into my hairline. It was unsightly and embarrassing!

I went through many prayer lines wanting desperately to be healed! Since the doctors could not handle this, God's healing was my only hope! The problem spread to my elbows and knees. Several times, I threw away my salves and creams just to prove that I had faith for healing.

One morning I was preparing to shampoo my hair and it always burned and stung. My head was over the sink and these words came into my mind, "There is no God." Why would I think something like that? I have believed in God all of my life! Then, other words came, "Even if there was a God, he does not give a damn about you." It was then that I realized where those thoughts were coming. The word "damn" was not a part of my vocabulary. I did not use that word! I wrapped the towel around my head and walked down the stairs, walked to the front door, opened it and cried out, "You dirty, rotten, lying devil! What are you doing in my house. You are not welcome here! There is a God in heaven! And He does love me! And even if I should die and go to my grave with psoriasis on my body, there is still a God and He loves me! Get out of my house!" I closed the door and continued my day.

I do not know how long it was, maybe a week or a little longer. I always had the habit of rubbing the back of my neck because of the continual itching. It was not itching and I could not feel any signs of that problem. I stopped. I turned around to Leon, lifted up my hair and asked Leon if he could see any psoriasis on my neck. He said that there was nothing there! I ran up to the mirror to look and I checked my body! I was healed!

Allergies: I grew up with food allergies, corn and milk. As I grew older, I begin to be very uncomfortable with the seasons of Spring and Summer—sneezing, coughing, eyes itching, nasal congestion! I begin to get allergy injections starting in January, one injection a month, and by March I was getting one injection a week, sometimes I would go in for a second injection and even with that, I was so uncomfortable. Even my breathing was hampered. The allergy specialist told me that I was allergic to all the trees, grasses and weeds in the Willamette Valley. He suggested that I should move to Arizona or Colorado.

It was the month of January. I was sitting at my desk at work (I worked for Georgia Pacific). I thought to myself that I needed to call for an appointment and begin my injections.

A thought came to me, "Do not take injections again, I am healing you!" I was excited!

I told Leon, and he replied, "Oh, honey, last year was your worst year. You are not getting better." I thought to myself, Leon is a man of God and he does believe, but he is not the one that heard those words. I did not allow myself to be discouraged or doubt. I did not talk about it, however, I did not have another injection.

It was toward the end of the month of June, the worst time when all the farms growing seed crops in the Valley were maturing and about ready to be harvested. A friend of ours, Ken Meyer, was at our house and he was suffering from the allergies—sneezing, coughing, blowing! He was so miserable! I was sitting on our couch and I lifted up my hands and thanked the Lord for His healing.

Leon looked at me and asked, "Did you stop your injections?" I told him I have not had another injection and I am healed! I gave that testimony to my friend! That must have been sometime in the 1980's, thirty plus years ago.

I have enjoyed the beautiful springs and summer times. I am so blessed!

THERE IS A GOD IN HEAVEN AND HE DOES LOVE ME!

I Remember...our thirty-fifth Anniversary

It was around the month of November in 1988. Our anniversary was coming up in a couple of months, JANUARY 10th. I said to Leon, "We have never done anything special on any of our anniversaries, not even our 25th, so let's do something on this next one". He asked me what I would like to do. Well, since it is in January, the middle of winter, I would like to go somewhere warm. Since we really could not afford a trip to Hawaii, I suggested that we could go south, like into Mexico. I thought some sun and water would be really nice.

I told him that I really just wanted some special time to ourselves and I was not interested in conventions or a pastor's conference, and then I whispered (so God could not hear me), "I really do not want to go to church! I do not want to pack church clothes. I just want to take cut offs, pants, tee-shirts and a swimming suit." Well, we started talking and thinking about where we could go.

About two weeks after this conversation, Leon received a phone call from Wayne and Evelyn Barron, missionaries in Mexico. They asked Leon if he would consider being their key note speaker for their pastor's conference. It was scheduled to begin on JANUARY 10th! Guess where we spent our anniversary? Up in the mountains in southeastern Mexico in a small town that sounded like "Thomason-Charlie". At least a 100 miles from the nearest beach.

We stayed in a hotel and the bed was a slab of cement with a 8-10 inch mattress on it. The only electric outlet was in the bathroom/shower combination. We enjoyed real Mexican food. We did not speak Spanish and very little English was used. We did not even know how to ask for water! I have learned since then the Spanish word for water, *agua*. (smile)

We had a great time! Leon ministered. We got acquainted with the people and enjoyed them! We were impressed with the work the

Barrons were accomplishing in Mexico and we were honored to be invited to be with them.

We were scheduled to go to Mexico City and have a lay over, so I talked Leon into just staying over in Mexico City for a couple of days. We took some tours in and outside of the city. We saw cathedrals that were built around the fourteenth century, and cities that were being excavated.

We learned a lot about the history of Mexico. The driver of one of the tour vans constantly told us about how the Spaniards had come into their country and conquered it. He talked constantly about how cruel the Spaniards were to the Indian people. The Native Indians became slaves to the Spaniards. The Indians were required to wear their shirts on the outside (not allowed to tuck their shirts inside), so that is when the women started cutting off the tails of the shirts and sewing them even around. A new style was being implemented!

During one of these tours, the guide had continually mentioned about the cruelty of the Spaniards, but he then said, "However, they did bring to us our religion."

I said, "Excuse me, you have talked constantly about how cruel the Spaniards were to all the natives."

He said, "yes".

I asked, "How could someone so cruel possibly bring to you a good religion?"

He did not answer and others in the van got quite. Leon gave me a nudge that meant for me to "drop it". I just wonder if it gave someone something to think about.

There were many shops in Mexico City that sold beautiful marble furniture! All kinds of marble tables. We bought us a marble coffee table and had it shipped home. It cost much more to ship than to buy. We still enjoy that table today and it has with it a memory of our 35th anniversary spent in Mexico.

As I have stated before, the Lord, it seems, constantly reminds me that this world is not a playground, but a battle field. We are thankful that God has chosen to use us in His army!

I Remember....My Personal Testimony

We had a group of young people from the Stone House in Boise, Idaho with us. They were young people that were saved during the "Jesus Movement".....hippies in the 1960's. They had been saved from drugs, alcohol, prostitution...the depths of sin.

One evening, we were sitting around in our home and one of the young men asked me about my testimony. I said, "Well, I guess I do not really have one." I told him:

I was raised in a Pentecostal Church, very strict, dress and doctrine ACTS 2:38 = SALVATION

My concept of God was that He is everywhere watching you all the time and had a big pencil and eraser. Every time you did something wrong, he erased your name out of that BOOK, and when you repented, he wrote it in again. Salvation was never certain, even after you had repented, been baptized and spoke in tongues. There was much condemnation and everything was a sin!

Lots of revivals that would last for weeks, lots of preaching about hell, I started going to the altar at a very young age and 'penting' and repenting. I would beg for the Holy Spirit with tongues. I was about seven years old and had a dream of Jesus coming...I was not going up to meet him and I looked ...I had on fingernail polish.

I was baptized in water at the age of eleven in Mangum, Oklahoma. My brother, Roy was baptized at this time, too. We were in the water at the lake. It was about 10:00 at night, a clear starry night. The evangelist said, "Look the glory of God must be with us." We looked and just above us was a small cloud. It did not move - just like it hovered over us. When the last one was baptized, the cloud just went up, up and out of sight. Then I received the baptism of the Holy Spirit at the same revival...walking out the door to go home. I hugged the pastor, "Grannie Overfield". I was so very happy to have received the gift of the Holy Spirit. The world looked new to me.

We moved to Harrisburg, Oregon when I was 13. My uncle, who baptized me, had moved to Harrisburg and started a church in the City Hall. I met Leon my first Sunday there. This was the summer before starting High School.

Leon was already aspiring to the ministry and we had a fairly large group of youth. Leon was the Youth Leader. We were not allowed to participate in very many school activities because everything was considered "worldly".

I was chosen to be class princess for the school carnival in the tenth grade. The pastors and elders did not approve, but my parents allowed me to do this.

Leon played basketball and was on the main five of the team... he was little but fast and was called the long shot artist. He could make a basket from the middle of the court. He had much respect of the team, coach and faculty. He was always asked to pray at special occasions and before games. The elders of the church didn't like him "parading around out there half naked" and insisted that he give up basketball or his position as youth leader. He quit playing in his junior year. Leon's dad became very disappointed toward the church because he was proud of Leon and loved watching him play basketball.

We stayed in the church and Leon served as Assistant Pastor until 1961 when his work moved us to Willow Creek, California and in a few years to Central Point, Oregon. We never really got involved in a church. About this time the Charismatic movement was starting and Leon would go to prayer breakfast. We had met a Nazarene Minister who had received the Holy Spirit. David Duplessis shared in one of them. My son, Ric, received the Holy Spirit baptism by the laying on of hands! Leon was also introduced to Watchman Nee's book "Normal Christian Church Life". He was faced with the question, "When are you saved?" This was way out of range from our teachings! GOD WAS SETTING HIM UP FOR CHANGE!

Our parents worried about us and thought we might be 'backslidden' because we had gotten involved with motorcycle riding, hill climbing competition and were not involved in church life. We spent most weekends involved in camping, fishing, playing on the motorcycles, etc.

The pastor resigned the church and Leon's Mother called and asked him if he would come on weekends a couple times a month until they got another pastor. We did this for six months. We had just built a new house in Central Point and had lived in it about eight months.....Leon felt he should go there and pastor the church that we had grown up in. Well, they loved Leon but I had changed. I had short hair, wore makeup, jewelry, my dresses were too short, even though they came to my knees, etc....Leon would receive letters telling him to shape me up.

One Sunday night he asked me to share whatever was on my heart. He had just been given another letter (from his mother) telling him that he would not ever succeed as a pastor if I did not make a change.

When we were leaving Central Point to come back to Harrisburg to pastor the church, I had a girl friend that made the statement, "I just can't imagine you playing the role of a pastor's wife".

I told the church that I had no plans to "play a role" because when you play a role, you pretend to be someone whom you are not. I said that I was not trying to please them and that I dress to please my husband.

I also told them to not expect my children to be examples for their children. You shape your own children up as needed. If my children are not following the Lord, I can't force them to be examples that you want them to be and it is possible that they are pleasing the Lord, just not pleasing you. I told them that I do have a relationship with the Lord and they should pray for me if they think I am doing wrong things and if the Lord deals with me, convicts me, I will change for Him or for Leon, but not to please them.

Needless to say we no longer fit in with the United Pentecostal Church and we really needed some fellowship. Leon was ripe when we met Brother Welch, founder of the Full Gospel Fellowship (FGFCMIO). The FGF is made up of different denominations. Even though I was rebellious about dress, I still believed the doctrine. It bothered me, when the IMA (International Ministerial Association) called Leon a compromiser....because he had fellowship with people of different doctrines and didn't try to change them. They dropped us from their fellowship.

It still bothered me. I asked Leon what he would do preaching at other churches that didn't know the truth, if someone got saved and the pastor did not baptize him/her in the name of Jesus but baptized him/her in the titles. He or/she would go to hell anyhow.......!

We could not just lead someone to salvation because if we didn't have a chance to teach them the doctrine and get them filled with the Baptism of the Holy Spirit speaking in other tongues, they would go to hell anyway.

My dream of Jesus delivered me from this bondage and I am thankful for this freedom!

I still wrestled with trying to be good enough to be saved and go to heaven. We were in a church service and singing, "When the role is called up yonder, I'll be there"...I received the revelation that I can never be good enough to deserve salvation. I will be saved because Jesus loves me!

GOD DELIVERED US FROM THE BONDAGE OF RELIGION AND WE ARE FREE TO ENJOY THE BODY OF CHRIST IN ITS FULLNESS!

Carla made her commitment to the Lord on her 16th birthday. Ric (age about 18) at a camp meeting during youth night said, "I am not a Christian but I want to be one. I have an ache in my gut that I want to be free from."

Our first missionary experience was with the Canadian Natives. This was the beginning of many experiences! When Brother Welch passed away, Leon was given the presidential responsibility of the Full Gospel Fellowship. We served as pastors at the Valley Christian Center for 15 years and have been in this position for 25 years.

We have had many experiences in many countries.....Mexico, Canada, Cambodia, Philippines (many places and different Islands) Africa (Zimbabwe, Kenya, Ghana, Togo, Benin, Nigeria) India, China, Malaysia, Venezuela.

After many years, I forgave the men in the IMA who treated us so badly....if they had not done this, we would still be in doctrinal bondage....It was a God thing.

One of my favorite Psalms: "How blessed is the man (woman) who does not walk in the counsel of the wicked, nor stand in the path of sinners, nor sit is the seat of scoffers, but his/her delight is in the law of the Lord, and in His law he/she meditates day and night."

We have been involved in "church stuff" all of our lives. We have not been perfect and I have not met another perfect Christian. However, we still believe and strive for God's best in our lives and desire to please our God and Savior.

God is still at work in me, causing me to desire to do those things that please Him. Phil 2:13

I have been loved by God!

Maybe I do have a testimony!

THE END

King David was the first one in the Scriptures to combine the words, "Hallel" and "Jah" which carries over into English and every other dialect as "Hallelujah". Therefore it is a one word international language.

In his letter to the Hebrews, Paul addressed those who were on the verge of turning back to the old Jewish sacrificial system of worship. "Jesus and the new covenant is superior," declared Paul, "and there is nothing to turn back to."

ISBN 1-4251-0272-7

Order on line:
www.trafford.com/06-2029 5120 97760

Book available at:
SW Badger Rd
Terrebonne OR

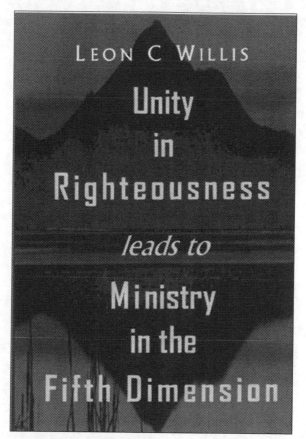

Ministry in the Fifth Dimension

The words, "Unity in Righteousness," were spoken to the author audibly at a time when little emphasis was being placed on the importance of Christian character.

As the church matures into the image of Christ, it will lead to "ministry in the fifth dimension." There are five levels of ministry, and the question can be asked, "What level of ministry do you function in?

Prophetic Insights

In the Old Testament there are types and shadows that give prophetic insights of the maturing church and the events that will take place before the second coming of Jesus.

Over the last 30 years God has given to me assurances that His Church will be the greatest force on earth, superseding any of the former world powers.

Jesus will remain seated in heaven until all of His enemies are placed under His feet, then He will descend with a shout, the trumpet will sound and the dead will rise!

Order on line:
www.trafford.com/06-2029 5120 97760

Book available at:
SW Badger Rd
Terrebonne OR

Keep your Head above the Stuff

What do you do when the "the stuff" of life causes your world to crumble? It happened to Joseph, David and Ezekiel and many others in the Scriptures.

There were fifteen places during the wilderness journey of Israel that challenged Moses. He dealt with forty years of "stuff", with only one slip up, and became a hero of faith.

Order on line:
www.trafford.com/06-2029 5120 97760

Book available at:
SW Badger Rd
Terrebonne OR

Road through Romans

In 1965 I was at a home gathering and a simple question was asked, "What saves a person?" On any other occasion I would have blurted out in no uncertain terms, "This is the way it is!" But something stopped me that night and I remained uncharacteristically silent, but the question kept rolling over and over in my mind, "What saves a person?" The Holy Spirit began to use material out of "The Normal Christian Life," written by Watchman Nee to counter what I had been taught for over 15 years.

A doctrinal revolution was started that night and the result was the writing of the "Road through Romans."

Order on line:
www.trafford.com/06-2029 5120 97760

Book available at:
SW Badger Rd
Terrebonne OR

Lift up thine Eyes

"Lift up your eyes" is a command by the Holy Spirit to the body of Christ. Because of the "doom and gloom" predictions about the future in the Christian community, it is imperative to shout out again and again, "Lift up your eyes", and see your opportunities to be useful in expanding the kingdom of God into all the earth.

ISBN 1-4251-0272-7

Order on line:
www.trafford.com/06-2029 5120 97760

Book available at:
SW Badger Rd
Terrebonne OR

ISBN 978-1-4251-6284-9

Order on line:
www.trafford.com/06-2029 5120 97760

Book available at:
SW Badger Rd
Terrebonne OR